The Day the Ship Knocked the Bridge Down

Where Were You?

By **Robert Hazel**

Chesapeake City, Maryland

11:38 A.M. – Tuesday, July 28, 1942

To The Favored

Those who told of when Schaefer's to Slicher's
Was a casual walk across a road-level bridge
That would sometimes lift them high
Above a town that was like no other

Acknowledgments

Many thanks are in order to the contributors of this collection of memories. Their kindness to me and their patient, thoughtful responses to my sometimes silly questions were extraordinary. Their hospitality was comforting, especially since my visits to talk may have come at inconvenient times.

Morrison Watson was especially helpful, with his valuable knowledge of the town. I'm grateful to Walter Cooling and Charles Wharton for their generosity in supplying wonderful, original photographs of Chesapeake City. I thank the many others who provided photographs and interesting items pertaining to Chesapeake City. I'm also indebted to Captain Ralph Hazel, who aroused my interest in the subject.

Introduction

I was tempted to call this book *The Last Days of Chesapeake City,* alluding to the book about the ancient Roman city of Pompeii, which was buried in lava and thus preserved for centuries. Thank goodness I resisted. In a strange way, though, their calamities affected Pompeii and Chesapeake City in similar ways. The *Franz Klasen*, our Mount Vesuvius, didn't bury, smother, and preserve our town for centuries. Yet the shock of its devastation flowed over us like lava, preserving the memory of that day in our minds for a lifetime. The question, "Where were you when the ship knocked the bridge down?", became an excavation, uncovering explicit activities of that day - buried by time - for us to relive.

Tanker after hitting bridge - South Side view

The destruction of Chesapeake City's lift bridge on July 28, 1942 was a spectacular event. At 11:38 A.M., after negotiating the curve near the pump house, the tanker, *Franz Klasen,* sheered uncontrollably to port and crashed into the south tower of the bridge. For the people of Chesapeake City who were old enough at the time, this event stands out clearly in their minds.

For them, it is similar in impact to shocking national happenings such as our entry into World War II, or President's Kennedy's assassination. Practically every person who was old enough to remember either event can tell you exactly where he or she was and precisely what he or she was doing at the time, sometimes with amazingly vivid details. The destruction of our lift bridge had the same effect on the residents of Chesapeake City. They all have different stories to tell - heard things differently, saw things differently, and remembered things differently. All who shared with me their impressions of that day did so with fervor. Their eyes sparkled; they spoke louder; they became animated with their recollections.

Our lift bridge was completed in 1925, and for a long while people called it "New Bridge." Its draw span was 260 feet long and the towers were 155 feet high. The total bridge structure weighed about 1,500 tons and the steel sections were two feet wide. The counterweights on each side weighed 300 tons each, equaling the 600 ton draw span. Constructed between 1924 and 1925, it opened for traffic in 1926.

Before its completion, to get from one side of town to the other, people would have to cross two bridges, High Bridge and Long Bridge, and part of the trip required traversing the rather long causeway between the two. My grandmother, Geneva Hazel, told me that she would sometimes, when in a hurry, walk across the locks, but doing that, she added, was a "foolish thing to do."

The opening of the lift bridge coincided with the new sea-level canal, which replaced the system of locks at Chesapeake City, Saint Georges, and Delaware City.

High Bridge - south view. This swing bridge crossed the canal at Hemphill Street on the North Side and connected with the Causeway, just west of the Pump House. Photo courtesy of Walter Cooling.

The bridge served the town well until that day in July when it was demolished, not to respond dutifully to the land traveler *or* the seafarer again. No longer would going to the post office, to school, to churches, to the movies, to the American Store, to the shoemaker's, to the drug store, or just to visit a friend be a short walk across town for North Side residents.

Those on the South Side felt the loss equally, for many friends and relatives, the fire house, churches, Schaefer's, and other stores and activities were located on the North Side. In addition, many South Siders worked north of the canal, in the Elkton area or in Delaware. Gone was the easy cross-town access both sides enjoyed. It would never return.

Long Bridge was a center-pivot span, operated manually with a crank. It connected Rees' Wharf to the Causeway. Photo courtesy of Mildred Alagia

A few of the following accounts of that unforgettable day are based on telephone discussions, but most are based on face-to-face conversations with people who were in or near Chesapeake City at the time. The conversations were held in the summer, fall, and winter of 1999. Where were you when the bridge was hit?

North Side view of bridge destruction – Note Lock Street, Bank Street, and Schaefer's store and restaurant

The day the ship knocked the bridge down – Where were you?

On Guard

I was in the service when the bridge was hit, but I received a letter telling me about it. We were in England preparing for the Normandy Invasion. Before I was sent overseas I was a soldier guarding the Chesapeake City Bridge for a while. I trained at Fort Meade and then I guarded a number of bridges in the Baltimore area. We would move from one bridge to another during the early part of the war. When I guarded our lift bridge we bunked in a small brick building located just as you got off the bridge on the North Side.

John Luzetsky – South Side, Chesapeake City, MD

Protected By Mom

My mother, my sister, and I had just walked off the bridge when it was hit. I was six years old and my mother was holding my hand and had my baby sister in her arms. We lived on Mt. Nebo and walked a lot in those days. My Aunt Mamie Moore lived on the North Side, in a double house across from where the Lum's used to live.

I don't remember hearing anything, but my mother did, so she grabbed me to protect me from the loud noise she heard. I remember her being frightened and wanting to shield me from whatever it was.

When we got to my aunt's, I know that she, too, was excited about the bridge being hit. I didn't go down to see the wreckage but later, riding the ferry, I could see the damage that was done. Of course, I did see a lot of photos of the ship and the mess that it made.

Audrey Kronemier Blevins - Elkton

A Head-on Collision

I was living at the time in the old Metz house on Saint Augustine Road. I was twenty three and married by then. I remember driving into town to get a haircut at Jim Humphry's barber shop next to the Rio Theater, and after the haircut I drove over to the pool hall next to Franklin Hall and went in to shoot some pool with some friends. In the middle of a game I heard a loud, crumbling crash that sounded like two trucks in a head-on collision.

We ran to the front door and I saw that the bridge was still weaving, and then I saw it fold down. It sort of folded itself or scissored down. I guess your mind sort of speeds up or something because it seemed as if it took a long while to fall, several seconds to fold down and fall, as in slow motion. I could only see the towers, not the draw span. The tower on my side I could see very well. Then I couldn't see it at all, because it fell and was hidden by Slicher's house and the Hole-In-The-Wall.

I walked down to look at it, past Slicher's and the Herriot Hotel and up the alley that was there then. There was a lot of confusion, people hollering and running around. My wife had been out the road and she was worried about me so she came in to see if I was all right. People from out Saint Augustine Road were coming in also, and I remember that they were very excited because they thought it was worse than it really was. For instance, one older lady was saying that the Germans had bombed the bridge.

West view of the bridge and the tender house. The old locks are in the foreground - circa 1930. Photo courtesy of Thelma King

I used to ride up and down on the bridge. We would climb up and crawl out and sit under the little tender's house which was in the middle. One time Jack Titter and I were riding the bridge - fooling around - and when the span came down Jack got his foot caught in the crack between the span and the road. He scrunched his toes back in his shoe so it didn't get him. He took his shoe off and had a devil of a time getting his shoe unstuck; he had to pull hard and wiggle it till it came out. We didn't want anybody to know what happened because we didn't want them to know how silly we were.

Sometimes we even climbed to the top of the towers. I remember one time, when I was below Jack as we headed down, being afraid that he would step on my fingers and cause me to fall.

Albert Clark - Newport, Delaware

Not Mr. Beiswanger?

When our bridge went down I was about five years old, and I was up at the school playing in that little alcove or U-shaped area where the basement steps was. We were fooling around there by the steps - Dicky Logue, a couple of other kids, and I - and we heard this noise. I recall that we were actually walking on the window ledge of one of the school windows. Well, we thought the noise was Mr. Bieswanger moving tables down in the basement. Now, that's the truth - my remembrance of it. The explosion wasn't tremendously loud or anything. It didn't even take us away from what we were doing.

We found out about it later, when we went downtown and realized that the bridge had been knocked down. Of course, by then there was a crowd of people all around. I don't remember what it looked like. I recall seeing the people all around and thinking, "My God, what's happened?" It was completely down then, and I think we were too afraid to get close enough to look at it.

Another thing I remember during that time period, World War II, was when the town sent air raid wardens around to each house at night to make sure people had their blinds closed. And a lot of people had black sheets or black material over their windows to black out the lights. The wardens were just guys from town. I remember that they wore white hats all the time. When the bridge was knocked down we lived in a double house on the South Side. Our house used to be right where that big bridge pillar is now.

Dick Sheridan – Hagerstown

The Sound of Thunder

I saw that lift bridge go down. One time I was down by the American Store - between it and the post office - on my bike, and Grason Stubbs came along and kicked my front wheel, which threw me off my bike. I fell down and broke every ligament in my knee. I remember that some man, in a real old car made into something like a huckster's wagon with wood on the side, picked me up and took me home. Then, a couple of days after that the bridge went down, and there I was on Nancy's bike with my knee all bandaged up so that I had trouble pedaling down to see the bridge damage.

When it was hit it make an awful crash - ka-BOOM. It was similar to thunder. I remember going down to see the ship that hit it. Mother was on the back porch shelling peas into her apron when the ship hit. Joe, my brother, was the one who called in to the newspaper. But we had an awful lot of fun riding up and down on it. Oh, we'd hear a ship blow and run down to the bridge and up to the top of it. Then, another time, Jane Sherman and I went down by Borger's wharf - where the water came in - and took Barcus' dog, Butch, with us. Well, we took Butch out onto the ice to play. Then, after a while, all of these whistles started blowing and people started yelling, "Danger, danger. Get off that ice!" They were frantic and we were oblivious to it all.

Jane Savin Thornton - Newark

Like Matchboxes Collapsing

I was a clerk in the office of the Corps of Engineers' building when the bridge was hit. Everybody in the building could see that the ship was veering off course and we all hollered and ran out on the porch and saw the bridge fall down right on the ship. It was just like matchboxes collapsing. We had a good view of it, there outside the office building; it's the same building that's there now, the dispatchers' office. I'm from Baltimore, and I got a job there in 1940. I worked there until September of 1942 when I joined the Navy. I remember some of the people who worked for the Corps: Ed Pratt, Bill Weaver (who worked in the storehouse), Miss Hollingsworth (who worked in the upstairs office), Mr. Sherman (the supervisor), Barney Ritter (a draftsman who worked upstairs), Rudy Taggart (who owned an apartment building on the North Side), and Harry Howard (who was related to Dr. Davis). They all worked there at the time.

We also heard shells going off when the ship struck. I think there were two shots that came from the gun on the forward deck. All of the freighters had gun aboard in those days. Then we all went down to get a close look at it. The ship was dead in the water with the bridge draped over it. I know it took them several days to get the iron off and to get the ship out of there. It was a mess for a while there - getting back and forth between the two sides, but eventually they got the ferry there and that helped a lot.

At the time, I boarded at the Bohemia Lodge on Bohemia Avenue. The owner was Evelyn Kibbler, a nice person. She kept things kind of straight there. We used to go to the Hole in the Wall and to Schaefer's a good bit. We rode back and forth on the ferry, and before the bridge was knocked down we used to get up on it, hide, and ride it up and down. I was just 19 years old at the time. After the bridge

went down we would ride anything that would take us over to Schaefer's. I remember riding the small passenger ferry a lot. I remember Mrs. Schaefer, John Schaefer, and a daughter. Bill Wallace liked her very much; I recall that clearly. She was young back then, but she'd be pretty old now, of course.
Claude Lumpkin – Massachusetts

I Screamed to Mother

When our bridge was hit I was sitting on the porch of our farmhouse on Saint Augustine Road. It made such a noise that I went out to look. It made a sound like metal scraping metal. I ran to our front yard and screamed to my mother that the bridge must be gone. I was twelve years old and it really scared me because the bridge tenders used to let us ride up on it when it rose to let the ships go through. I rode it up a couple of times. Of course, my parents never knew it. Yes, the workers would take you up occasionally. When the roadway went up you could hear machinery running. I don't know; it wasn't a real loud noise or anything, just the chains hoisting it up.

You know, when I moved to Baltimore to go to school, I met a fellow who was on the ship that hit the bridge. He was one of the sailors on it when they brought it back to Baltimore. It was a German ship that hit the bridge, I believe. He said they wouldn't let him off the ship after it hit. I met him in 1949, and he told me that it was quite an experience. He explained to me that those aboard were not allowed out, that they had to go with it when they took it back. His name was Frank Mills, and he was a friend of my husband's.

When the ferry was running I was a young teenager; we kids had a lot of fun riding back and forth on it. We would walk on and go upstairs, just for something to do. I had friends on both sides of the canal; we got together for fun on the ferry. I remember how it would sometimes bump up against the pilings on the way in. But that always happens when boats come in to dock.

My father was Stanley Stevens, and he had a farm that extended from town - where the creek ran in back of Bohemia Avenue - to the area on both sides of Saint Augustine Road. Our land went out there quite a distance. I remember a 1939 panel truck that he had; I loved that thing. I used to cut asparagus for Dad. The field towards town was full of it. I remember some great things about the old town: Schaefer's, Bieswanger's, Postell's, and the Rio Theater. Every Saturday afternoon we'd go to the movies. We'd see the Tom Mix cowboy movies and all those crazy things.

Margaret Ann Stevens Kruger – Catonsville

Joined at the Hip

I didn't see or hear the bridge go down because I was too far away. We didn't move into town from our farm until January, 1943. I was twelve years old when the bridge was hit. We went in to see the damage. It was a weird sight for a kid my age - a ship there with the bridge on top of it. I had crossed that old bridge many times to see my sister who lived in Elkton. Sometimes we would have to wait because of a ship going through.

The *Gotham* came into service in 1943, and until then we had to ride a small boat back and forth to school. It was a nice little boat ride. When the wind was strong and when a ship was coming through, the crossing would be delayed. I remember how Miss Crowgey, one of our school teachers, used to leave her car on the North Side and take the small ferry to school. The boat used to pull in at City Dock on the South Side.

I rode the big car ferry, the *Gotham*, to school, also. Sometimes, in cold weather, we kids would ride the ferry just to get warm. We would go upstairs to the passengers' department and lean up against where the smokestack came through. High winds would often cause the ferry to lose control and bang up against the pilings. For us kids this was a big thing.

I was a friend of Edward Sheridan, who was Capt. Ed's son. The Captain would let us go up into the wheelhouse. My best friend at that time was Buddy Carlton. My mother used to say that we were joined at the hip. The *Gotham* was still running in 1947 when I left Chesapeake City.
     Clifton Ginn - Nebraska

A Terrible Noise

I was living on the South Side when the bridge was hit. I was kind of young then, but I remember it. It really made a terrible noise, like something hit something else hard. I didn't see it go down but I saw the damage later, not right away because I was frightened at first; everybody was. We lived over on Charles Street when it was hit. In fact, they put one of those piers right in our back yard. That's why we're here on Bank Street; Daddy had to move. They took a lot of houses here on the North Side also. But I saw the bridge down that day. The towers were down and the ship was there, damaged. It was there quite a while before they took it away.

You know, people used to ride that bridge up. I did too, but only one time. I just screamed and hollered. A man and a woman - Bernie Carter and his wife, May - who lived in the little house next to the church - took me up on the bridge. As it went up, Bernie said, "It won't hurt you, Mary," and I said, "No, I know it won't hurt me because I won't be able to get off." But I recall how I just screamed so much, and they were patting me on the back, trying to calm me; I was little. But I never went up on it again. It made so much noise going up; that's what really frightened me. It made a deep, whirling sound and I sure didn't look down, not even once.

Mary Jackson Watson - North Side

A Rising Rust Cloud

I was at home that day, here on Saint Augustine Road, across from Mr. Leon Swyka's blacksmith shop. My brother and I were taking the stairway down in our mother's house. I heard a noise - like dynamite going off, a big thud. When I went outside and looked towards the bridge I saw that it was gone. I saw a rust cloud rising where the bridge had been.

John Trush - South Side, near Chesapeake City

Down in the Hole

I was born in Elkton in 1941, so I don't remember when the bridge was destroyed. But I do remember living along the canal, next to the old wooden structure that was used for a firehouse. We lived on Biddle Street and I remember the Brezas, Betty and Charlie. I'm surprised I remember that because I was only five at the time.

Now, I remember that ferry. I traveled across it many times. In fact, I recall hearing a woman on our street say that she certainly wouldn't ride that small, replacement ferry across that canal. That ferry was smaller and not very good in that swift tide. She used to yell, "I'm not riding in that thing!"

I spent a lot of time on my grandfather's farm on Randalia Road. His name was Alex Hotra. We fished and crabbed in the canal, and we used to cook the crabs with the water that we took right out of the canal. I have a lot of great memories about Chesapeake City. I used to ride my bicycle down and get on the ferry. I don't recall riding in a car at all. What I'll never forget was when I fell into the hole that they dug to put the bridge in. It was 1946 when I fell in and I was scared to death. When I got out I was all muddy, and I remember going down to the river to wash my clothes because I was afraid of getting my butt beat. I was told: "Don't go down there where they're working." I remember almost drowning at Basalyga's wharf one time. The current took me and Uncle Joe Hotra had to pull me out.
Emil Chicosky

Like the Sound from Aberdeen

When the bridge was hit we were on our way home from Elkton. My dad was driving and Margie Stubbs was in the car with us. We were right about where Miss Spear lived, on the old road, when we heard the crash. My dad said, "I know what that is. I'm going to take you girls home." He told me to stay with my mother while he went down to take pictures.

Later, I think my dad took me down to see the destruction, but I don't remember much about it. I know that the ship hit the tower that was closer to the South Side. We didn't see the bridge go down but we sure heard it. The sound was like what you hear coming from Aberdeen - a big, loud thud. I can remember it as plain as day. We were in Dad's black Chevy.

My dad, Earl Sykes, was the bridge tender at Summit. Everybody loved and respected my dad. When there was a thunderstorm, I used to pray that my father wouldn't get hit by lightning. He used to do things for people and never asked for anything.

Gertrude Sykes McNeal - Elkton

It Shook and Trembled

I was looking at the bridge when it was hit. I was on Sisters' Hill, by the orphanage there, so I had a good view. I heard the rumble of the bridge going down; it was like thunder, and I looked and saw the bridge above the trees. It shook, trembled, and went on down. Then all of us kids started yelling, "The bridge fell down; the bridge fell down."

After the bridge was destroyed we had to take that launch to school. I didn't have to walk far but the Aldersons really had a long walk from their farm in back of the shipyard. I was six years old at the time. Then they brought the *Gotham* down, and I remember that the pilot's name was Bus Browne. Occasionally we kids would get to ride up there in the wheelhouse as we went across. That was quite a thrill even though it was such a short ride. And, I think that it was in *Ripley's Believe It Or Not* as the shortest ferry ride that sometimes needed an icebreaker to get the ferry across.

I can remember riding up on that lift bridge when I was real young. On our way to church, my mother and I would ride it up, and I'd look down at the ship stacks as they passed under. And I watched the military ships go by during the war. Also, looking back, I recall that at the same time they were putting in the ferry slip they were also taking out the old locks. Part of the locks was still left when the canal was widened, and they took the last of it out when they prepared for the ferry.

Charles Breza - Elkton

Roll Out the Barrels

I was living in our double house on Cecil Street, near the ball park. I heard a sound like barrels rolling down the street - a rumbling noise. I knew something bad had happened so I ran down to Mary's, my sister-in-law's. She told me that the bridge was hit and she was afraid that her two sons, Junior and Buddy, were on the bridge when it was hit. People - mainly kids - would sometimes ride up on the middle span when it lifted for a ship to pass under. The bridge tender would chase them but the kids would hide behind the steel structures. I then ran down towards the bridge to look for my nephews. When I saw the fallen bridge and the twisted black steel on the ship, I got frightened and ran back home.

Miriam Ohrel - North Side

The Dream

I was working in Elkton at the time, when somebody came in and told me that our bridge had been hit. My father was on the North Side, not far from it when it came down. He predicted that a ship would destroy the bridge. I dreamed that our bridge was going to be knocked out, and the next day the Saint Georges bridge went out; two people lost their lives up there. That was in 1939 and after that they moved the operators to a control house over on land, on the South Side.

The *Victory,* a small passenger ferry, which operated until the *Gotham* became available - Fall, 1942. Photo courtesy of Corps of Engineers.

When I finally came to look at the wreck I saw that the ship was over toward the South Side, and all of the bridge structure was down; much of it was on the ship. Then we had to take the small ferry, which my father, Captain Cooling, piloted. Lots of times people who lived on the South Side would keep their cars on the North Side, ride the small ferry boat, and then use their cars to go on to Elkton or other areas north of the canal. Other than that they'd have to go all the way around Summit. The small ferry would dock there where they just put the new floating dock, and people would walk up between Reed's store and

Conrey's store, which is called Franklin Hall now. They built that ferry slip road quickly; it was all marsh, which they had to fill in first.

Beginning construction of the lift bridge - south view - circa 1924. The concrete piers had to be dynamited out in the 60s. Photo courtesy of Walter Cooling

But getting back to the bridge, when I was a boy I used to ride up on it. I'd go up in the little house with the operator. In fact, when they were building the bridge, I used to climb up it, up the towers. Of course you had to do it after working hours, you see, and one evening I climbed up there with another boy, and I climbed high up there - not quite all the way to the top though - and I looked around and he was nowhere to be found. It may have been Frank Briscoe but I'm not sure.

Then, after the bridge became operational, the operator would let me climb the ladder which led to the little house and let me ride up and down a few times. They weren't as safety-minded as they are today. I think the operator's name was Lloyd, but I'm not positive. It didn't take much trouble to raise the middle span because the big weights on each end weighed about the same - it balanced. And, yes, my father was standing right next to it when it went down. He had told people well in advance that a ship would take it down, and then it happened.

I also remember the steamboats that used to come through here. As a kid I used to jump off them into Back Creek. You see, we kids used to swim off the V, which was a wharf area at the entrance to the Chesapeake City Locks. The locks were next to Schaefer's old store. Well, if we saw the *Penn* or the *Lord Baltimore* in the locks, ready to drop into Back Creek, we would run up there, climb aboard, ride it a short distance, and then dive off into the water. Nobody on the boats ever objected.

Walter Cooling - South Side

Hanging on to the Side

Of course, I used to walk across that lift bridge. In fact, I used to ride up on it. The bridge tenders didn't say anything. We used to hang onto the side of it as it moved up. We wanted to see how high we could go up before we let go. Now, when it was knocked down

I was working on the *Manhattan* dredge. We were dredging down around Crystal Beach, and the news of it being hit came over the radio. By the time we got back to Chesapeake the ship was gone, but we could see the damage; that's for sure.

You know that wharf that the government had at Town Point? Well, the Ericsson Line Company put that in out there so their steamers could tie up. They had a 99-year lease on it. Sure, I went to the Town Point one-room schoolhouse. Gertrude Manlove was our teacher. I went there with Murray Bowers, Billy and Ruth Purdy, Bill Purner, Ruthy Broadwater, the Mindosas, Charley Bailey, the Sheldons, and the Bakeovens. There were four of us Johnstons: Daisy, Arthur, Gertrude, and myself. They closed the school down when I was in the Sixth Grade; then they bussed us to Chesapeake Elementary.

Murray Bowers tried to knock the foundation out from underneath the Town Point School one time. He used a sledgehammer on it. You can still see the damage to the wall if you go look at it. It's on the side facing the river. He did a pretty good job on it. Another thing I recall is that we had a coal stove in the middle of the room. Well, one day Murray threw a bullet into it and busted it. It was quite an explosion - scared all of us. But we kept right on using it. Murray didn't go to school there long, but he didn't want to go at all; that's why he did those ornery things.

Robert "Snake" Johnston - Smyrna, Delaware

False Alarm

I was six years old and living in my family house on Biddle Street. I was in the alley in back of our house, working with my mother in the garden, when a neighbor told us that the bridge was hit. Bus McCool drove over and picked up my father in his car. They thought that Melvin, my twelve year old brother, was riding up on the bridge when it was hit. Mr. McCool took my father to the wreck and consoled him for losing his son. Then they discovered that Melvin was not on the bridge but was playing somewhere else.
Jack Lum - South Side

Fuzz Was Flying

I was crabbing on the South Side between the Bayard House and Mallory Toy's pool room. I saw the tanker with the four tugs come by and they were headed towards the south tower of the bridge. Then everything happened at once. Men started yelling and started chopping the hawsers with axes, and from all of the fuzz flying up in the air I knew something was going on. I just stood there watching. I had six or seven crab lines out on the little wharf there, and they had a big wooden barrier around the bridge pier. I kept looking when all of a sudden the ship came through the barrier and hit that pier. POW! Here she come.

Dredging in the 30's - west view. Photo courtesy of Walter Cooling

    I was next to Johnny Walter's boat ramp and I remember more than anything else the whistles blowing and the fuzz from the rope - all of that hemp - going up in the air. There wasn't any nylon back in those days. I just stood there and I didn't know what to do, whether to run or I don't know; it happened so fast. As I said, all of the men started hooping and hollering and cutting the big hawsers with axes. Those ropes were as big as a man's arm. Then all of the men started running down the center aisle of the tanker towards the stern. And those tug whistles were blowing like mad. The whole upper bridge came down and after they got everything loose the ship didn't go on to Baltimore. They had to take it back to Philadelphia. It sat there about a day and a half.

Francis Brown - South Side

Too Close

I sure can remember when the ship hit that lift bridge. I was close to it - too close. I was sitting on a bench out in front of the building where, later on, Walter Coleman had a poolroom. I recall that I was eating ice cream that I had bought from the little store next to Nichols' shoe store. I can't recall who owned that little place. Now, when that bridge was hit I was scared. I took off. I thought those Germans were after us. And the rumors did spread that the Germans took out the bridge to close off the waterway and so forth.

Pete Swyka - North East

Working at Postell's

When the ship hit our bridge in 1942, I was working at Postell's. They had sent soldiers to guard the bridge. They were there even before it was hit, and I remember that John Luzetsky was one of the soldiers.

When that ship crashed into the bridge it was as if a bomb had been dropped. I was still in high school at the time and things didn't mean that much to me. In my house we didn't have a newspaper or a radio, so we thought, "O.K., the bridge fell and nobody was killed." It wasn't that important to us.

Mary Boyko Tarabochia - California

A Cannon Going Off

When the bridge was destroyed I was standing on Back Street, or what they now call Charles Street. What I heard sounded like a cannon going off, a booming sound. I didn't see it hit, but when I heard the noise I ran down the street towards it. It was so long ago. All I can remember is that it was something big out there in the water.

I can barely remember the small boat that hauled people across the canal after the bridge was knocked down. The ferry I remember best is the big *Gotham*. I was riding it once when a dog jumped off into the water, just as the boat was leaving the South Side dock. Well, the dog was drawn into the propeller and killed.

I learned to swim right there at City Dock. Whitey Whiteoak shoved me overboard so I had to. My father, Pop, told me a lot of things about the old town. He said that the Rees House, which is now the Inn at the Canal, was built because Brady was going with a woman, and he told her that if she married him he'd build her a fine house. And that's what happened. It used to be brick, but then they put German siding on it. Pop said that they had to get their water from somewhere up on Third Street, where they had a well. Pop also told me about Joe Savin's wood shop, which is still up there, behind the big white house where Dr. Davis' office used to be. Pop said that

when he was a boy they had a great big work horse, and when it died they dug a huge hole inside Joe's shop and buried the horse in there. Tommy Vaughan owns the building now, and I suppose the horse's skeleton is still under there.
John Eveland, Jr. - North Side

I heard a Crash

I was home at the time, in the white house on the corner of Third and George Streets. Dr. Davis had his office there also. I was in the kitchen feeding the baby when I heard a crash. It wasn't too loud so I wasn't very concerned. Then I went outside and saw that the bridge had been hit. Dr. Davis had one of our children with him. He was out making a call at the time of the collision.

When Dr. Davis returned, I remember that he treated a man who was injured when the ship struck the bridge. The man was under guard because it was wartime and the ship was from Germany. Some men from the Corps of Engineers brought him to the office. Dr. Davis examined him and found that his injuries were not serious, just some bruises and possibly some small pieces of metal in his skin.
Eloise Davis - South Side, Randalia

Sneaking on at Night

Yes, I do remember when the lift bridge was hit, and I know I wasn't on it at the time. The old Rio Theater was by the canal, near the bridge, and sometimes in the summertime, when it was hot, we'd come out of the movies and Jack Titter and I would get on the bridge and ride on it. We rode up on it a lot of nights. After a while they didn't want people to ride up on it, so we had to sneak on at night. We went to the movies every Saturday night.

When I was a kid we owned the farm that went right down to Hollywood Beach. I remember when the Ericsson Line Steamers used to stop at the Town Point Wharf. In fact, we used to ship tomatoes from that wharf. Yes, I watched those steamers run up and down the river. We used to go to Philadelphia on the Night Boat. We'd board at the wharf in Chesapeake City at 10:30 and get to Philly real early in the morning. I wasn't tired when we got there because we always got a berth.

Bill Briscoe - Galena

Snake on the Bridge

When the bridge was hit we lived on Canal Street, which has now been torn out of there. When the ship hit, it made such a noise that we all ran out to see what it was. It sounded like an explosion. When we ran down to look there wasn't anything left.

I know that when the ferry was running I worked for Archie Crawford. He used to take off and leave me there to mind the store and pump gas. I remember Schaefer's store and restaurant, also. I worked fifteen years for John Schaefer. He was a good man to work for. One of those bartenders thought he was king of the hill. One time, he reached over and patted me, and if it hadn't been for John Schaefer he would have been wearing the drinks I had in my hand. As soon as he touched me John hit him.

Yeah, the old Schaefer's was good times. We had great fun there. I remember that somebody put a live black snake in one of the trash cans. We all knew that Bill Reynolds was terribly afraid of snakes, and it was his job to take the trash over the bridge to the dump. Well, Bill loaded the trashcans into his pickup and started up the bridge. About halfway up the lid jostled off and the snake came crawling out. Bill stopped the truck then and there and jumped out to get away from that snake. He just opened the door, leaped out, and left the truck and garbage up there in the middle of the bridge.

Norma Merchant Kelly - Near Town, North Side

Running Mothers

Well, I was living on the North Side at the end of Canal Street, and I had just turned six years old so I don't remember much. I heard a noise and then my mother and all of the mothers on the North Side of town, including all of us kids, ran en masse down Canal Street as far as we could. I thought I heard shells exploding from the ship.

Raymond "Birdy" Battersby - South Side

She Had a Fit

I was riding my bike on Saint Augustine Road, where my grandparents lived at the time. I heard a booming sound and I was looking towards town so I saw it fall. It went down fast, I think. I was very excited and sped to tell my grandmother. "Mom, the bridge is gone," I told her. 'deed it is!' she said, and then she started hollering. She had a fit because she thought her husband, Tom, may have been on the bridge. She wouldn't let me go anywhere near town.

Tom Newlin - North Side

Unexpected News from Home

I was somewhere in the Atlantic, on my way to Wales when our bridge was destroyed. By August we were moving around England and France, preparing for the invasion of North Africa. We weren't sent there but we were getting things ready for it. I got a letter from my mother in early September. She told me that the bridge had been destroyed.

David Biddle - South Side, near Chesapeake City

What's In the Pot?

I was home at the time. We lived in the double house on Cecil Street, across from Taylor Stubbs. I heard a terrible noise, like bombs crashing; we thought we were being bombed. I was inside the house when it happened. I remember that my mother had wanted me to go over town to the grocery store but for some reason I didn't go. I'm glad I didn't. There was so much confusion that day that women preparing dinner didn't remember what they had put in the pot.

Anna Schrader - North Side

Puzzled Nuns

I was next to our church on Basil Avenue, in school with the nuns when the bridge was hit. We kids ran towards the bridge to see what had happened. The main thing I remember was that the nuns were upset because they didn't know how they were going to get home to their convent on the North Side.

Alex Luzetsky - North Side, near Chesapeake City

A High-Pitched Noise

We kids were swimming in the canal, skinny dipping probably. We were on the North Side, down from where Reynolds had all of his carnival rides stored. I heard a crunching sound and a screeching, high-pitched noise like iron against iron. I was ten years old at the time, and when I looked towards the sound I saw the bridge go down. It seemed to descend in slow motion. All of us kids ran down, and I saw the middle part - the part that went up and down - lying on the bow of the tanker. The south tower was stretched out almost flat against the ship. The men wouldn't let us get too close though.

Aftermath of the collision, with the Pump House in the distance - east view

For a year or so before the ship hit the bridge, the soldiers would guard it with their rifles because it was wartime. I remember that the school teachers had their students put on a little show to entertain the soldiers. They sang some songs during one of the holidays.

Frank "Tots" Sheldon - North Side, near Chesapeake City

Awakened by the Racket

When the bridge was hit I was in bed because I had been working the night shift, and I heard this terrible racket. It was warm weather and the window was up, and I saw all this smoke and debris in the air. I got in my '39 Ford and ran in there to see what happened. It was a bad scene, too, because the Germans were sinking many ships out there on the coast. Many of the ships were coming through the canal so the German submarines couldn't get to them. But the noise of that crash was something unusual, very unusual for Chesapeake City.

Allen Purner - Elkton

I Felt the Ground Shaking

I was eight or nine when the ship collided with our bridge. We children were up at the Hall, the Ukrainian Hall on Bohemia Avenue where we were having class. I think somebody came in and told us. But I remember feeling the ground shaking. We went outside to see what happened; I knew it was a hard impact. Then we kids all ran to the canal to look at it. I don't remember but we must have seen part of the steel from the bridge actually on top of the ship. It was a terrible day, really.

Then they brought the ferry in; it was here for quite a while. I have a picture of the ferry with Jeanette Sheridan, Doris Williams, and me standing by the railing on the top deck of the ferry. We girls used to ride it just for fun. We'd go after school and just ride from one side to the other before we went home. Those were the good old days, actually. Capt. Sheridan, the pilot, was Jeanette's father. I was good friends with Jeanette, used to stop for her every morning on the way to school.

Barbara Blendy - South Side

A Lot of Whistles Blowing

The most exciting thing that ever happened in our town was when the ship hit our lift bridge. I was seven years old and in my back yard when I heard this racket, a screeching and scraping, God-awful noise, like a hundred-car wreck - very loud. And to a young kid in our quiet, little town, it sounded like the end of the world. Then I looked towards the noise and saw the south tower fall, followed by the north tower's collapse, and then I heard a lot of whistles blowing. So I ran down there and there it was, the big ship with the bridge on top of it.

Then I ran back to tell my grandmother, Bessie Tatman, about it because I knew she'd be upset, and I saw my father coming out of the store with his camera. He ran down and took a lot of pictures, but the police took his camera because they didn't want pictures taken because of the war. This is funny because I don't have a good memory about the past, but that bridge wreck is just as plain as if it happened yesterday.

Gary Tatman - New Castle

Running in My Pajamas

Yes indeed, I remember when our bridge went down. We lived on Canal Street, right next to the Thornton's. The noise woke me up. In fact, I ran down there in my pajamas. It was a loud crash that scared me half to death. It happened in the morning. I was in bed because I was probably working the night shift somewhere. Now I remember; I was working the 4-12 shift at the Triumph Plant. Yes, I ran down there and I recall seeing the boat with the bridge down on it. Then I ran all the way back home. It seemed as if everybody in town went down there.

I remember riding the ferry. My husband, Jule, was in the service and George Beaston used to meet me on Canal Street because I was afraid to walk down that dark street.

Betty Merchant Bristow - Florida

Jumping from the Lift Bridge

I was working away from Chesapeake City when the ship destroyed our bridge. My mother was working at Schaefer's at the time so she would remember it well. But I was probably driving a truck up on the levee. I did go down to see the damage. It was an awful looking mess down there. We had to go around Summit until they brought the ferry here.

I used to jump off that old bridge and swim all around that area. We'd ride it up as high as we wanted to go before jumping off. They'd blow the whistle when they were going to raise the bridge, so we would know when to get on. The bridge span didn't rise up very fast; it was a pretty slow ride, really.

I had to walk over that bridge to go to school. I tell people that I had to walk back and forth to school uphill ... both ways! And that's true because I would walk down Spear's Hill from Stubbsville and then uphill to the Sisters'. Then I would walk down Lock Street, over the lift bridge and uphill again until I reached the school. We used to ride over the bridge in a car, also. And, of course, sometimes we had to wait for it to come down.

I remember how I used to go with my mother and father to the dances that Roy Foard used to have in a room over his hardware store. They had a little band that played every Saturday night. There was always a good group of dancers there. My parents didn't have a babysitter so they had to take me along. I'll always remember sitting there and watching them all dance around.

Eddie Stubbs - Stubbsville

Crumbling Paper

I was on the front porch of our house next to the Presbyterian Church on Biddle Street. I heard whistles blowing on the boats, tug whistles I think, and then a noise, not very loud though. The sound must have been muffled by the water. Then I saw the ship hit the bridge. I just looked - amazed. The bridge then fell slowly, like papier-mâché crumbling. It sort of fell in on itself, like a building that they blow up from the inside. It was surprising that the bridge crumbled into the water instead of just falling over. My husband, Archie, said, "I might as well close my doors." He thought his garage business was finished, but then they brought the ferry in.

Helen Crawford - South Side, near Chesapeake City

Crab Bait

I don't remember when the ship hit that bridge, but I do recall riding the ferry and when the new bridge was built. My dad used to persuade a guy on the ferry to play his accordion and sing as we cruised down the river. At the time, we lived out on Randalia Road, and I can just remember riding the ferry in the wintertime, and how we'd get up against the wall where the exhaust stacks came through so we could get warm. We'd ride for no reason, just for fun.

I remember that it was during that time period when a man jumped off a ship to commit suicide. It was a while before they found the body. Well, my dad helped pull him out of the water. And, do you know, he was all covered with crabs; he didn't look too good.

The town has changed so much since the ferry days. I remember a guy named Al Pettigrew. Al had a barbershop alongside a sub shop on Second Street. If you came off the ferry on the South Side and made a right turn, his shop was on the left about halfway up the hill. I used to get a haircut for fifty cents. And then get a sandwich next door. He owned both shops, and I think he had a reputation for being shady. I was in there one time when he pulled out a .22 pistol and started shooting at a guy's feet. The guy's name was "Salty Dog." Anyway, the pistol had blanks in it but Salty Dog didn't know it so he was dancing all around and hollering.

James Sullins - Middletown, Delaware

A Tangled Mess

When the ship hit our bridge I was in the back yard hanging up clothes. It didn't make much of a sound; maybe I just didn't pay any attention to it. I remember, before it was hit, that the National Guard checked every truck that went across each way. I was eighteen - just out of high school, and I used to walk back and forth over the bridge. Daddy also used to drive us over in our 1939 Dodge. I remember taking the Bungards, who didn't have a car, for a ride one time, and we had a flat tire just after we crossed over the lift bridge.

But, yes, I eventually walked down to see the damage that was done to the bridge. It was a tangled mess, almost like wartime destruction. It's frightening to think that a lot of kids used to ride up on that bridge. They would have been killed that day, of course. I never did ride up on it though.

I graduated in 1942, and I hadn't gone to work when the bridge was knocked down in July. My mother thought I never was going to work. But then, in August, I started working in Aberdeen, and I used to ride my bike in to my aunt's, get on the ferry, and ride to the North Side where I caught a Greyhound bus to Aberdeen. It made a lot of stops to pick up people along the way who also worked at Aberdeen. I remember missing the ferry one time, so my father and I hitchhiked clear to Aberdeen. That was during World War II; people wouldn't take a day off.

Emily Givens - South Side

Will You Marry Me?

I was in Postell's corner store, there on George Street, and I heard this terrible noise. It sounded as if a big army truck had flipped over and slid down the road on its side. That's the best way I can describe it. I walked down to the site to have a look, and I said to whoever was there with us, "Where's the bridge?"

Then I saw the ship there, and what was left of the span draped across her bow.

We were living in Chesapeake City at the time. We had moved there from Pennsylvania over the Christmas holidays that year. The bridge was hit in the summertime, so I would have been out of school. I used to work part-time for Luther Postell, and I was working that day. I walked down to get as close as I could to the accident, but there were soldiers guarding both sides of the bridge and they wouldn't let you get too close. They also wouldn't anyone take pictures.

Yes, I remember when the ferry ran. In fact, in the summer of 1948, my girlfriend, Ann, and I and some friends of ours were riding the ferry on our way back from Rock Hall. And, as we were making the crossing, I thought to myself, "I've always wanted to propose on the water; I'm going to do it right now!" So I proposed to her on that ferry. We had met on a blind date and had only known each other for a couple of weeks. But she said, "Yes!" and we've been together ever since.

As I mentioned, I used to work for Postell while I was in school, especially in the summer. I worked at two of his locations. One was called the Jiffy Grill, which was near Elk Forrest Road, and the other one was at the Bohemia River. They were sort of predecessors of McDonald's; I guess you could say. Postell sold a number of items: hot dogs, hamburgers, root beer, and so forth. His root beer was in a big barrel, mixed with syrup and seltzer water. My job was to mix the two together, a certain amount of syrup to a gallon of seltzer water. I have good memories about living in Chesapeake City. I used to swim in the canal many times, right off the dock down from the Bayard House. I jumped off the dock many times.

I worked in town on an ice truck with two Chesapeake City boys, Albert Fithian and Bob Gilbert. I was helping them because they had a great deal of ice to deliver to local dairy farmers. We worked for the Elkton Supply Company, which was on the corner across from the Rio Theater. Bob was older than Albert and I and he was drafted into the army. Albert enlisted in the Marine Corp and I enlisted in the Navy. Bob was killed in the Battle of the Bulge and Albert was killed on Okinawa. Their names are on the memorial stone near the Methodist Church in Chesapeake City.

Kenneth Wilcox - Elkton

It Started Weaving

i was working the late shift at the New Castle County Airport. When I got home Eleanor and I went over to the South Side to get the mail. When we approached the bridge coming back, the bells were ringing and the gates were down, but when the operator saw us he raised the gates back up, waved us on, and said, "Go ahead." Then when we got back home we heard a loud crash; all of that steel and the concrete counter weights made a racket when they hit the ship and the water. When the ship hit the concrete abutments the bridge started weaving and down it came. I used to ride the thing - stand right in the middle - and I used to think, "Boy this would be a bad place to be if a ship were to hit."

Ralph Northrop - North Side

A Part of Us Gone

When the drawbridge was hit my husband, Ralph, was standing on the canal bank, not far from the Hole in the Wall. I wish I had had a camera, but we didn't have money for cameras in those days. I went across that bridge many times. In fact, my mother and I crossed it to go to the Elkton Hospital when my son, Ralph, was born. He was born in the old Elkton Hospital. We caught the bridge but Dr. Davis didn't; he had to wait for it to come down. We were worried that we might have to wait at the bridge. My water had broken at Town Point Road, and my mother said, "Oh, man, I hope we make it!" Well, we made it and went bumpily, bumpily, bump across.

Now, when that ship hit it, Ralph had just walked outside from shooting pool, and was on his way to our house when he heard the noise of the bridge going down. He saw the ship there and came running to our house on George Street (which was owned by Joe Savin and was right across from Beiswanger's). He grabbed me and said, "Come on; I want to show you something." It was remarkable ... but I wish we had had a camera because we were right there, almost on top of it, there at the end of George Street. It was terrible because it was part of us gone.

After that, Ralph and I used to ride the ferry all the time. When I think of the ferry I think of Ralph and me together when we were young. George Shestock told Helen Breza, after Ralph passed away, that Ralph Eveland was crazy over that girl (meaning me!). That was when I came into First Year High, and Ralph told George, "I'm going to get *her*." And George told him, "Don't be so sure; there're other boys in here, you know." So, we started going together in Second Year High. We went to the Rio Theater a lot, and I had to be home right after the show was over. Anyway, my parents finally approved of him and we had a great, happy life together.

I remember hearing about an awful fight on that ferry one night. A Chesapeake City man got beat up badly. The man who got beat up was a drinker. I knew him very well and was really scared of him. Anyway, one night he fought with a sailor, and if people hadn't stopped it the sailor would have killed him. The sailor had his head and he was slamming it up against that big, heavy chain. Well, he got away from the sailor and got home somehow. Ralph and I went there to see if we could help. He really smelled badly of alcohol and was covered with blood. I know that he didn't fight after that; that cured him of fighting *and* alcohol.

My brother and I went to the one-room schoolhouse at Town Point. His name is Robert Johnston, but everybody calls him "Snake." I'll tell you how he got that nickname. Gertrude Manlove, our teacher, couldn't get her car started one afternoon after school. So Bobby said, "Let me look, Miss Anna. Maybe I can find what's wrong." Then he said, all innocent like, "Oh, Miss Anna, there's a snake in there wrapped around your coil." Well, he had put that snake in there to be ornery. So, from then on everybody called him "Snake." But the teacher never found out. Now, I know that Miss Manlove did a great job of teaching. She taught the First Grade to the Seventh. We were all in groups and everything went very well. I remember some of my schoolmates: Ruth Ginn, Virginia Purdy, Frankie Ulary, May Briscoe, Fred Rothers, Dorsey Johnson, The McConney girls, the Griffin boys, and all the Whitlocks. The really ornery one was Lewis Whitlock. We were scared to death of him.

Gertrude Johnston Eveland - North Side

A Big Racket

I was outside of my shop here on Basil Avenue. I heard a big racket, a loud noise. It was the ship hitting the bridge, and I would say that the bridge went down fast. The steel fell on the ship and took her bow down. Later, when the men were clearing the metal from the wreckage, I saw one of the steel links and asked if I could have it. The guy said that if I could lift it I could take it home. So I lifted it. The link was from one of the chains that lifted the bridge span. It was oval-shaped, about a foot long, eight inches wide, eight inches thick, and very heavy - over a hundred pounds I would say.

Paul Breza - South Side

Running Scared

I was working in Elkton, doing plumbing work in the new Hollingsworth Manor project. In the morning of the day it was knocked down, Paul Harris was going up the street with a keg of nails on his shoulder. Well, he knew Milton and me so he hollered down to us: "I heard that the bridge was just knocked down in Chesapeake. Cannons went off and the windows were shot out of houses." Of course it was a rumor. No guns ever went off; nobody ever heard of that. But we expected our bridge to be hit after Saint Georges; it wasn't a shock.

By the time I got home the guards were there and they wouldn't let you get too close. I got just about as far as where the Presbyterian Church is on Biddle Street. All you could see was the ship and part of the bridge lying across the bow. They tied one of the tugs that accompanied the ship over at Schaefer's and the other two they must have tied up at City Dock. John Schaefer was sitting on Catherine's front porch and looked right at it when the ship hit. He started having his arthritis attacks about that time and he was sitting in a rocking chair. He told me that the bridge came down just about like an old erector set.

It was common knowledge, pretty much, that John Schaefer was concerned about a ship hitting the bridge, especially after that freighter destroyed the Saint Georges bridge in 1939. John was afraid that the north tower might hit his store. He instructed his dock workers to run in and tell anybody who might be in the store to get out of there fast if a ship started to ram the bridge. People inside, of course, would not have been able to see it coming.

(preceding picture)
View from the lift bridge of the Schaefer's store and restaurant - circa 1940

There's another thing that happened when that bridge was hit, according to Harry Pensel. Clarence Truss, Charley Booker, and Harry were working on John Schaefer's pier. Charley Booker was on a pile driver that was tied to the pier, and when the bridge started falling - and the noise it made - caused somebody to yell, "Look out!" Well, Charley Booker was so excited that he took off running through the little shack on the pile driver instead of running down the deck where it was clear. He just about tore all of the skin off of his shins and knees. He ran into everything inside the shack as he ran through it: gears, levers, benches, and other machinery. Harry Pensel said he ran into all of it on his way through.

Note shack on the span, where operators stayed until 1939. In that year two men were killed when a ship hit the Saint Georges' lift bridge. After that, operators stayed on the shore.

Pretty girl on the bridge walkway - circa 1935. Photo courtesy of Thelma King

Looking back, I remember well how when we were kids we used to run to jump on and ride the bridge up. We'd hear a ship blow and dash like mad from the Elkton Supply area or in front of the movie hall down to ride her up. But the last time was with Pepsi Benson. We rode up - that was after the Saint Georges bridge was knocked down - and I said to myself, "If I ever get down off this son of a gun it'll be my last trip up here." You can imagine what it would be like if a ship hit that bridge and knocked it the heck down with you on the span.

I can tell you that each bridge had a foreman who was in charge of the whole bridge and all of the tenders and everything else. They had an office right there as you came off of the bridge on the North Side, where the battery house was. It was the same building where the soldiers stayed when they guarded the bridge. It served as an oil shed, battery house, and so forth. It was next to George Knott's office.

Morrison Watson - North Side

Tangled Bridge

I had just stepped out of the kitchen door when I heard a loud noise and looked up just in time to see the bridge come down. It was an upsetting sight, so astounding to see all of that metal falling on the boat. The bridge fell suddenly, quickly; I couldn't believe that it could have come down in that amount of time. It was so massive.

There may have been guns going off but I'm not sure. I was dumbfounded; my mouth gaped open. I couldn't believe it. There was a lot of commotion because everybody ran out of their homes to see what had happened. We rushed down to the canal, about a block and a half away, and saw that the bridge itself was tangled and lying on the ship. It was sad, the end of an era.

Evelyn Morgan - Cecilton, Maryland

All Muddy

I was about six years old and living on Biddle Street. I remember that I was playing in a mud puddle in front of Archie's old filling station. It was across the street from his more recent station on the corner of Biddle and Hemphill. I heard a noise and then people started running towards the bridge. I went down and saw that it wasn't there.

Freddy Rhoades - North Side

The Sound of Music

I was getting gas at Elkton Supply, which was on the corner across from the Rio Theater. I had just got away from the station on my way to Bethel when I saw the ship coming. Then the bridge went right down on the ship's bow; it didn't fully disappear but fell on the ship. By the time I got back to Bethel everybody knew about it. That ship stayed there for quite a while. Sometimes we could hear music coming from it. At first a government tug was used to take people across. I believe Frank Briscoe worked on it. I know that later they dynamited the bridge piers out of there.

Earl Schrader - North Side

Metal Scraping Metal

I was at the homestead on Basil Avenue, next to the Saint Basil's Church. I was just a kid in my bare feet and I was down in back playing in the field when I heard a loud noise like metal scraping metal. I looked towards the noise and I saw that the bridge wasn't there. I ran like mad up Pop's cart road and then ran to town, down Basil Avenue and past Sager's. When I got to the canal I saw the bridge on top of the ship. A lot of people were there and there was a lot of confusion.

Nicky Luzetsky - North Side

Bridge in the water, with *Franz Klasen* in the background. photo courtesy of Morrison Watson

A Screeching Sound

I was in my back yard on Saint Augustine Road. I was between the summer kitchen and barn when I heard a big metal booming sound, along with a loud screeching and crumbling sound of metal on metal. I ran right away into Chesapeake City as far as the old

Elkton Supply station, between Postell's and the movie theater. So many people were there that I couldn't see anything, so I climbed up Mary's Beaston's beauty parlor steps.

I was little, only seven years old, and I remember that someone kept grabbing my hand to keep me from jumping around so much. Finally I was able to see that the bridge was down and that a black ship was there. I have vivid memories of pieces of metal twisted sideways, the collapsed towers, concrete abutments, and strange noises. I could see that the ship was listing and turned sideways in the canal.

Al "Junior" DiGirolamo - Lakeworth, Florida

Banging Chairs Together

When our bridge was hit I was in Laurel, Delaware, visiting my aunt and uncle. When my uncle told me that our bridge was knocked down, I thought he was teasing me. I said, "Oh, it did not." And he said, "I'm telling you the truth." I remember Bobby Sheridan telling me that when it was hit he was out in the yard by the school, and he thought the noise was Mr. Beiswanger banging the chairs together. Mr. Bieswanger was the school janitor at the time. I saw the mess when I returned to Chesapeake. But when we were kids we used to walk across that bridge all the time; we thought that was something.

Jeanette Sheridan Miklas – Charlestown

Bombs Going Off

I was swimming in the canal at the time. We were on the North Side, east of Archie's, down the bank from where Earl Wralston lived on Canal Street. I heard sounds like two bombs going off; they were shells exploding on the bow of the ship. We kids ran home like mad we were so scared. I went later to see the wreckage; all of the steel was crashed across the bow. That ship stayed there for a long time before it was moved.

Frank Elwood - South Side

Hold the Lima Beans

I remember when the ship hit our bridge. I was sitting here in the living room, hulling lima beans. It was a loud crash. I believe that a man was killed on the bow. Then, for a long while we had the ferry here. It took us across the canal - north to south and south to north. It was nice. It carried cars and passengers, and every fifteen or twenty minutes you made the trip.

But I remember Long Bridge and High Bridge. High Bridge was a swing bridge. And when I was a little girl we used to sneak on it and ride it as it swung around. Long Bridge had to be cranked open from the middle. It was a center-pivot bridge. Those were good days.

Ella Norris Savin - South Side

A Moment of Hysteria

I was inside our house, the big one on the corner of Hemphill and Cecil Streets, when I heard a huge, loud, cracking noise. There was a minute or two of hysteria, for we knew that something awful had happened. When we went outside we saw that the bridge towers were not there. My mother made me go back inside so I would not see any gory sights. She wouldn't let me go near it because it was so frightening.

Alma Gleason - South Side, Port Herman

A Real Disaster

When our bridge came down, a friend of mine and I were on vacation. I was living in Chesapeake City at the time, but Ruth Ginn and I had gone away on vacation. We heard about it when we were down there and said "Oh, my!" When we returned we saw what happened to our bridge. It was a disaster - a disaster. The damage was so bad that we weren't allowed to get too close to it, you see.

We really had fun riding up on that bridge when we were kids. Every time the whistle would blow we'd run to get on it. I remember how old Earl Sykes would holler, "Off of the bridge, off of the bridge!" He was kidding us kids, you know. Earl was the bridge tender. Yes, we'd make a bee-line to the bridge and

he'd yell, "Off of the bridge, off of the bridge you Ticktowners." He always called us Ticktowners.
Doris Savin Farlow – Newport

Ironing in the Street

I was in Aberdeen at the time. When I got home my mother told me about the ship hitting the bridge. She was ironing clothes in our home and shop, B.F. Nichols Shoe Repairing. The shop was next to the Rio Theater and very close to the lift bridge. She heard an awful crash, and was so excited that she took the iron out in the street with her. She told me that she screamed when she saw what happened.

View from the bridge of South Chesapeake City. The large building is the Rio Theater - circa 1940. Photo courtesy of Charles Wharton.

When I got home I saw the mess. The steel bridge had collapsed and had gone on the ship; it was lying on the ship, not the same as when the Saint Georges bridge was hit. I was in Saint Georges and saw the ship hit that bridge. The steel came straight down and fell, not hitting the ship. The steel reacted differently because it was a cold day in January. The Chesapeake City bridge was hit on a hot July day, so the steel collapsed right on the bow.

    I expected that a ship would someday destroy our bridge, because of all the close calls. I remember standing on George Street, close to the bridge, and watching a ship sheer out of control and collide with the bridge. I saw it coming - moving slowly, drifting slowly - till it scraped the bridge but didn't take it down. The cables rattled and shook; it was scary. They constructed fenders to protect the bridge, but they didn't help when that tanker smashed and took it down.

    I used to ride up on that bridge. Before the Saint Georges bridge was hit they would let us ride. On Saturday evenings the steamer, *John Cadwalader,* would pass under and many people would sometimes ride up so they could look down on it and all of the passengers aboard. Sometimes there would be so many people on the bridge that the tender would come out and chase some of them off. Two of the bridge tenders were Friday Rhodes and George Knott, the boss. They didn't care if we rode the bridge.

                Bob Nichols - Elkton, Maryland

Bubbles Popping

I was sitting in a rocking chair on the porch of the Bayard House. I heard a loud popping noise, as if someone was popping the plastic packing bubbles that protect items sent through the mail. But it was loud and frightening. I ran into the Bayard House and didn't come out. Later I saw the wreckage, the ship and all of the twisted black steel from the bridge.

I remember talking to Doris Austin about where she was when the ship hit our bridge. She said that she was visiting Edna, her sister, who was married to Frank Bristow. She had Edna's little girl, Sandra Lee, in a stroller and she walked across the bridge to the South Side to get groceries at the American Store and to talk to me for a while. Then she had to get back to Edna's with the groceries, and do you know that she was the last person to cross that bridge before it was hit. She said that, as she walked on the bridge, she heard the ship's whistle blow and had to run with that baby across the rest of the bridge. She remembers ducking down under the gate to get through. When she got to Edna's, which was close by, Edna came out to help with the groceries and the baby, and they heard this awful crash of the ship hitting the bridge. Doris said that Edna started crying and said, "My God, you and Sandra Lee could have been killed."

Ester Luzetsky - North Side

John Breza viewing the bridge from the Herriot Hotel porch, with Schaefer's store above the protective pilings - circa 1932. Photo courtesy of Monica Breza

A Loud Thud

I was trimming a hedge row at the Durham Farm when I heard a loud thud. And I knew right away that a ship had hit our bridge. It was wartime and there were many, many vessels sailing through our canal, and I thought it would be only a matter of time before one would hit it. Saint Georges Bridge was struck a few years earlier and two men were killed. Bill Oaks was the bridge tender who was killed, because at that time the tender house sat right on the center span.

After that they put the house on the ground, away from the bridge. That's why our man wasn't killed. I was too far away to see that the bridge was gone, but later on I went in and saw all of the damage. The bridge roadway was lying across the tanker and the old stuccoed operator's house was shattered and in the water.
Harold Lee - North Side

Everybody Running

I remember when the bridge was hit. It was in 1942, and we went down to look at it. Things were a mess down there, very crowded, with everybody running to see what was going on. The ship was still there, and all of the steel from the bridge.
Dorothy Loveless Stubbs – Stubbsville

Hanging up the Diapers

At that time we were living in the apartments, next to Archie's filling station, when it happened. I was in the back yard hanging up my baby son's diapers, when I heard a rumbling noise, and when I looked I saw the bridge crumbling. The middle collapsed on the ship. Then I went in the apartment, got the baby, got in the car, and went on around over Summit Bridge to check on my father, Bill Purdy, who was a guard on the bridge. He was there when the bridge was hit, and when I found out that he wasn't injured I was very relieved. *Ruth Ginn - North Side, near Chesapeake City.*

Lucky To Be Alive

    I was standing by the dock on the South Side. I lived in the last house on the row, right there close to the canal. There was a little restaurant there, a butcher shop, a place where they sold coal, and a weigh station for when the boats came in with oysters, grain, and other goods. That dock is where we used to swim so much, and I remember getting into all kinds of trouble jumping off the ferry when it came in.

    When that ship hit the bridge my little brother, Frankie, and I were right there on the dock, and when it went down it scared the heck out of us. Then he started crying and started asking me how Daddy and Mommy were going to get home. He didn't know about Summit Bridge at that age. I was about six then, and I saw the ship coming when it was right about where the water wheel is. When the tug lost control, you could see the ship sort of veering off, and the tug was trying to get control of it when it ran smack into the South Side abutment. The first thing that toppled was the left tower, and then the middle just came straight down.

    When the tower fell on the bow of the ship there was a man standing there, and that big ring or pulley fell right around him. The tower on the other side just fell on top of the whole mess. That's why the canal was all jammed up for so long. Ahhh, it was frightening. There were several guys on deck; they were lucky to be alive. The ship was kind of floating free and they were trying to get control of it. As I remember it, it looked as if the bridge fell in slow motion, and then things really started popping. It was just like dominoes the way it came down.

It was a German ship and as soon as the Corps of Engineers could get there they painted over the name really fast, because that was during World War II. But there was a curve there at the end of the North Side, and I remember clearly that a line snapped or something and the tug lost control of her; the ship was coming ahead of the tug and the tug was trying to pull back. One of the tugs on her was a big sea-going vessel out of New York. I can't remember the name of the towing company but I think it may have been the Loveland Line or the Big M Line. But the ship was under some kind of power, and, with the strong current and the line snapping, it just shoved her right into the bridge.

The sound when it hit is hard to describe; it was the grinding, screaming sound of metal on metal when it starts to twist. There was a loud boom when it fell, like a bomb going off. The best way I can describe it is like when I was in Korea - something blowing up beside me. But I'm pretty sure there were no shells or bombs on the ship. It was a captured German freighter, so it wasn't armed. But the impact jolted the whole dock. I was dumbfounded, standing there looking at all this - and whoa! I didn't try to get any closer to it because stuff was still falling from the tower.

I used to ride that bridge when it went up. The tender's name was Paul, and he used to get on my case all of the time because when the bridge was going up I'd climb up on the left-hand abutment and dive off. I'd also climb up into the towers, all kinds of screwy things. Man, don't make me think about all of that stuff. When the new bridge was half finished we'd walk all over it and slide down the top of that big arch. We'd climb inside of that silly thing and hide.

After the old bridge was knocked down, it took four years to clear all of the debris out of there, and it took a while to move that ship out of there; things were completely blocked there at Schaefer's. I remember now that men were yelling before the ship hit, and, yes, the whistles were blowing at least five or six times, and then they'd let up and then start blowing again. I know because that was what startled my brother, Frankie, so much. And the most amazing thing was how that giant pulley - it had to have been as big as this room - crashed onto the bow of that ship with the sailor standing right in the middle. He wasn't hurt, but when it crashed all around him he froze, stone cold; he couldn't move.

That ship stayed there for a while, but it didn't take them long to put the ferry road in. The area was a swamp, and when they were building the road they lost a bulldozer in there; it sank in the muck and they couldn't get it out. I watched it; it took two days for it to sink but it finally disappeared.

Grason Stubbs - Elkton, Maryland

No Excuse for It

When our bridge was hit I was working at Bainbridge; I had just got out of school in '42. When I came home that evening I found out that I had to drive around by Summit Bridge. The ship was headed west, and it ran into the south side of the bridge. I went down later to look at what happened and saw that the bridge was buckled more from the South Side of Chesapeake than it was from the North Side. I don't believe anybody was hurt when it went down. I don't remember much about the operation of cleaning it up, except I heard that the ship's captain was laughing about it. I don't know if it's true or not. But the damage was some sight to behold. I don't think there was much of an excuse for their hitting the bridge to start with.

Thomas Foard - near town, North Side

Down the Smoke Stack

I was working at the Dover Air Force Base for the Philadelphia District Engineers out of Chesapeake City. My friend and I were on our way home in a survey truck and when we got near Salmon's Pond I said, "The bridge is down" and my friend said, "What do you mean, it's down?" And I said, "It's not up there anymore; it's knocked down." So he said, "How do you know?" And I answered, "I don't see the two towers there anymore, where the counter-weights hold on." So, sure enough, we got in there to the government office and as soon as we did they asked us to go out there on a catamaran and take soundings to see how deep the bridge was sunken down there so some boats could go through. They wouldn't let us go home; we started working right away.

    To take the soundings we used a piece of lead and a line that had the feet marked off on it and, well, it would be wrapped with something. We'd drop the lines down there until the lead hit and they'd blow a whistle and we'd pull the lines up, take readings, and sound off what the depth was. We'd drift with the tide. See, we'd have about a half dozen catamarans hooked up end for end, whatever it would take to cross the canal. There were outboard motors on the end ones. The whole idea was to tell which sized boats could go through there, depending on how much water they would draw.

    I remember when the locks were there. That was when Pop worked for the government. He worked on the old locks, and we kids used to walk across the bridge and walk around there and Pop would be down there and I'd wave at him. He used to work on the waterwheel too, by the government office there. He had to repair it sometimes. I remember standing on the bridge span, and sometimes at low tide it was so shallow that I could see mud on the bottom. But little by little the Corps dredged it out and made a canal out of it.

Dad told me that when they were deepening and widening the canal at Summit, when he worked over there, they had a thing that would hold the mud, and they would take it and dump it into dinkies. Well, Dad knew that it was a poor method but they wouldn't listen to him. He said that one time the contraption grabbed a laborer's arm and ripped it off. This happened at the Summit, where they had a covered bridge so they could get the horses to cross the water. In fact, we had some boards from that old bridge. They were exactly sixteen inches wide and a full inch thick. I wish I still had them. Some of them were even two feet wide.

But when our bridge was hit they moved the ship right away; it didn't stay there long. The steel span was all over the ship and, do you know, we rode that bridge span a lot when we were kids. One time a ship hit one side of it and shook it while we were up there. After that they wouldn't let us ride any more. The bridge tender would chase us off. Yes, we used to watch the boats and ships go through below, and I remember that Pete Harmer would take these big matches and drop them to try to make them fall into the smoke stacks. Pete was good at that. The stack was pretty big and he'd take that match and drop it and it would go right into the stack; sometimes he'd miss, though.

Nick Swyka—South Side, near Chesapeake City

I Was Frantic

I was washing the lunch dishes at my mother's house on Biddle Street extension. I heard an awful crash; it was so unexpected and I was frantic because I knew that my grandfather, Charles Cooling, was at the bridge. I ran down and saw all of the collapsed steel on the ship. I found out that he was all right but he was very upset. Before the bridge was hit he saw the tanker sheering with the current towards the south end of it. He ran away from the bridge as fast as he could. Some people blamed the accident on the pilot because he didn't have much experience.

Frances Lee - North Side

Banging and Clashing

I have a vivid memory of the day the lift bridge was demolished. I was just a kid and lived near the canal, pretty close to Schaefer's Restaurant. I was sitting on the front porch shelling lima beans when the bridge went down. I was just sitting there when I heard all the banging and clashing, so I walked up towards the bridge towers and saw that they were gone. I didn't know what it was at first when I heard all of the banging and so forth. You always thought the towers were going to be still standing, but they weren't. And I didn't hear any guns going off, as some people have said. I heard a loud, clanging noise. It really brought back memories of when I used to ride the drawbridge up and down. Other kids and I would run and get on it so we could ride it up and watch the ships go under. You weren't supposed to be on there, but we did it all the time.

Fortunately, nobody was on it when the ship hit. I went down to Schaefer's store and looked around at the damage. I could see the bridge structure lying over the ship. A little later on, they blocked everything off so nobody could get close. The ship had had tugboats on it; it was not under its own power but was being towed through. The tugs didn't have the power to keep the current from taking the ship into the bridge. It was a German tanker that had been captured. It was wartime and they had had soldiers guarding the bridge. They were housed in a little brick building on the North Side of the canal.

John Conley - Elkton

Shooting Out Fire

When our bridge got knocked down, I was sitting down at the water's edge playing in the sand, right down here past the one-room Colored schoolhouse. My mother attended that school before I was born.

Anyway, I was there in the sand and all at once I heard all of this noise: ba-LOOM. I looked and saw the bridge falling on the boat, and I jumped up and ran home to tell my mother. She was asleep because she had worked the night shift at the plant. And I yelled, "Mom, the bridge just fell down." And she said, "Doggone it, get out of here, telling that story." "I'm not kidding," I said, and kept raving about it so much that she finally came out and walked down to take a look. But I still recall how loud it was when it came down, and then it started smoking, with fire shooting out.

Steve Warwick - South Side

Quite a Sight

I was a kid, of course, but I remember when the ship hit our bridge. Dad took me down to look at it. The bridge was lying across the bow of the ship. We looked at it from the North Side, right there by Schaefer's store. My dad worked for the government, and for a while he bartended down at the Hole-In-The-Wall.

Jimmy Stubbs - Dearhaven

Worried About Getting Home

During the war, the lift bridge was hit by a ship. My husband, Harry, was across the canal at the time, and he saw the ship hit it. I recall being worried about how he was going to get home. I heard him say that he rode up on the bridge when he was a boy. He told me that his brother, Taylor, dived off it. Harry worked for the Corps of Engineers. He was on one of the dredges that worked on the canal and in the Delaware Bay. He worked shift work.

Madeline Sykes Stubbs – Dearhaven

A Loud Crack

I was playing on the North Side, behind Archie's gas station. There was a wooded area back there and I had climbed a tree. I heard a loud crack, a sound of steel twisting when the bridge was hit by an old tanker. We were kids and weren't allowed to stray too far from home, so I didn't go down there. I saw it later, though, with all of the steel lying on the ship. I have a note that Albert Moore wrote when it happened. He worked for the Corps of Engineers and wrote down: "The bridge has been hit."

Dwayne Biggs - North Side

A Pile of Junk

I was twelve years old when the lift bridge went down. I didn't hear the crash because I was on the farm, probably running the tractor. I did go in to see it piled up down there. It looked like a pile of junk. I talked to one of the guys who was on the ship that hit it. The bridge accident was just after Pearl Harbor, and I've heard that when the bridge was hit, the women in their houses were getting dinner ready.

And when they heard the crash they left their stoves on and their pots on the stoves and ran right down to see it.

I remember when my third-grade teacher, Mrs. Walter Cooling, I believe, walked our class across the lift bridge. We had been studying trees, so she made an appointment with either Brown's Lumber Yard or Short and Walls; we had to go over and look at the lumber. She had us kids walking two and two across there. Well, I was OK until I saw the opening around the abutment going down to the water, and then I had to walk on the inside, next to the road. I couldn't take being too close to the water.

Ted Lake - near town, South Side

Yes! I'll Marry You!

That summer, when the bridge was destroyed, I was working in Elkton. I was just out of high school - about to start college in the fall - and I had a job with an insurance that paid $12.50 a week. Anyway, we heard about the bridge, and one of the secretaries in the office had an old car, so we went down after work to have a look. Well, we could see that it wasn't there but we couldn't get close enough to see the damage.

The end of that bridge brought the ferry, and I recall something great that happened aboard it. Kenneth, my husband-to-be, and I had just met a few weeks before, and we were on our way back to Elkton from Rock Hall with another couple. Well, as we were moving across the water, he proposed to me. I thought about it for a while - I thought he was crazy! That was in August, and we were married that same Thanksgiving. He was in college on the GI Bill, and that was the first time he was able to get a few days off.

My father, David Frazer, worked on the *Weir* and the *Dragon*, tugboats that serviced the canal. I think he started that job in 1934, when William Taggard was the chief engineer for the government. I remember that my father worked with Roy Diebert and Roland Cooling. Another thing I recall is that it was during the Depression, and my father received a Christmas bonus of $5.00. Well, the check blew overboard into the canal. For some reason, that really stands out in my mind. Daddy was very familiar with the river because he and my grandfather had had a cabin cruiser docked in Elkton, and when I was little they would take a lot of people for cruises down the river and through the canal every single Sunday. But, when the Depression came, that all ended.

My husband, that summer he lived in Chesapeake City, worked on the ice truck for Elkton Supply. He had two friends working with him: Robert Gilbert and Albert Fithian. They all went into the service after that. Bob said, "I'm not coming back." And he didn't! Ken was the only one who lived through it.

Ann Frazer Wilcox

I Felt Like Crying

I was at home here on Chestnut Springs Road so I didn't hear or see the bridge go down. I walked everywhere in those days; we didn't have a car. The day the bridge went down I remember walking in towards town and I was looking for the bridge towers, watching for the towers as I walked, but I never saw them. You know, I felt like crying because later on as I walked I heard people saying, "The bridge is down," but I kept looking for it anyway and couldn't find it. I was always used to seeing it as I walked into town.

View from the South Side - circa 1935. Photo courtesy of Walter Cooling

I was working at Schaefer's as a waitress at the time but was off that morning. After the bridge went down, John Schaefer would send his little boat to the South Side to pick us up so we could work for him.

The boat would pull up to get us near the Herriot Hotel. From where I worked at Schaefer's I could see the divers working to open up the canal, to get all of the things out. The divers and other workers used to come in and out of Schaefer's restaurant, and lots of sightseers used to come into the restaurant just to look at the damage - the bridge down in the water.

John Schaefer and his sister were very good to me; he was very charitable and good to everybody. He had a ship's chandlery as well as the restaurant. I knew Mrs. Schaefer, Winifred, John's mother, also. Her maiden name was Schmitt. She used to make deviled crabs in her home. She used the original crab shell which she'd fill up with crab meat and cook in deep fat and serve with French fries.

Years ago I used to walk across that old bridge a lot. I went over it many times in a car, also, on my way to the Elkton railroad station. I also used to walk over the locks sometimes; I was scared stiff going across. I used to go to the Saint Rose church on the North Side.

Monica "Mamie" Breza - South Side, near Chesapeake City

Distraught Mother

Oh, Yes! I was only four but I remember how distraught my mother was on that day. She was worried that my brother, Junior, was crossing when the bridge hit.

Dolores Carlton Hazel – South Side

Walking across the lock gates - circa 1926.

I Watched It Swerve

I was not living in Chesapeake City when the ship hit the bridge, but Clarence Truss, whom I call "Uncle," told me about it. He was a carpenter and was building a pier for John Schaefer when it happened. He saw the ship coming and told me, "I knew that danged thing was going to hit. I watched it swerve out of control and sure enough." That's all I know, what Uncle told me.

Thelma Buckworth King - Smynra, Delaware

My Bed Shook

I certainly do remember the day the ship hit the lift bridge. I was in bed asleep. That was during the war and they covered the name of that ship up right away. It was the *Franz Klasen*. Marie Savin and I were friendly with the soldiers who guarded that bridge and the general area. I was living with my grandparents, in a house that was just a block from the firehouse. As I said, I was in bed when the bridge was hit, because I was working night work at Triumph Explosives. They had buses taking people from all around to work there. I was great friends with Alma Carlton, and we rode to work with Mr. Morgan.

    Anyhow, when that ship struck the bridge, our house shook and my bed shook. I thought we were being bombed. I really did. It was so loud. I got out of bed to find out what was wrong, but I don't remember what I did after that. I do know that we were worried about our soldier friends because they were down there so close to the accident. But nobody was badly injured. I recall hearing a man say that on his way home from Elkton that day, he looked up to see the top of the bridge towers but they weren't there. Normally, as you approached Chesapeake City, at a certain point, you could see the bridge. He said that it was such a strange feeling to look up and not see it. I went down and took pictures of the collapsed bridge and the ship. I don't think the ship was badly damaged. They got it away from there pretty soon, because it was a German ship. Most of the fallen steel was on the South Side.

    You know, when the boats approached the bridge, they'd blow three times for the bridge to go up, and I remember one time when I was going across. There was an old black lady who was starting to walk on the bridge to go over town. Well, she didn't hear the three blasts from the boat, so I told her that the bridge was going to go up and that she should get off of it. I was afraid she might fall over the edge as it was going up. She thanked me for telling her, and another day, when I got home, she was sitting in our kitchen with my grandmother. She had a quarter for me for saving her life. That accident was really an inconvenient thing for us because we had to ride around over Buck Bridge, which was about ten miles, just to go over town.

Frances McCoy Williams – Newark

Down the Manhole

I was sitting on our front porch when the lift bridge was hit. I heard the four toots of the tug and realized that some danger or something was happening. So I ran out into the street to see what it was, and just as I got out there, the left side of the ship hit the south tower and the bridge just fell right down on the ship. I ran down toward the bridge and those cables were coming down and hitting the street, and I heard a noise down there like steel falling. I saw old George Knotts, the bridge tender, run down those steps and up the street as fast as he could. To me, as a kid, it was comical.

Pretty soon the army came over from one of the forts to evacuate the town. They thought the ship may have had ammunition on it. But it turned out that the only ammunition on it was for the forward gun. And, as I recall, the only person who was hurt was the guy riding up in the bow. He dove down the manhole.

Joe Savin, Jr.- California

No More School that Day

I remember when that ship took our bridge down. I was in the church hall, there on Basil Avenue. The sisters were teaching catechism classes on that day. I know that Alex was laughing about the sisters, because they had no way to get back to their home on the North Side. You could hear that loud boom for miles - really loud, with all of that steel coming down. We kids all ran down to see it: Helen and Alex Lutzetsky, the Yonko boys, my sister and I.

There were about twenty of us and we all ran down to see it. We saw everything because we were there within fifteen minutes of the collision. I remember running past the movie theater. After that, the day was over. We went home, no more school that day.

Joe Hotra - near town, South Side

Echoing Up the Canal

I remember when the bridge fell. I was about eight years old and was out in the yard and I heard this terrible explosion. I said, "Oh, my God," and ran in

the house. But we didn't know what it was. I thought somebody dropped a bomb because it was during the war, you know. We lived on a little farm on the North Side and when the bridge was hit I could hear the sound echo up the canal. It kind of jarred the ground, sort of what a bomb would do. That's what it felt like, anyway. Of course, I was only eight years old, but it did shake the ground like an earthquake. But I didn't know then that the bridge had been hit. I used to ride over that bridge in a car. I remember the big, concrete weights which would raise and lower the center span. Sometimes we had to wait in line until a ship went through.
Richard Johnson – Bethel

Somebody Bombed the Bridge

I had just crossed the bridge in my truck with a load of ice when that tanker hit it. The whistle had blown but they waved me over. Mine was the last vehicle to cross on it, I believe. I pulled into Mom and Dad's driveway, there across from Taylor Stubbs, and I heard everybody hollering that somebody bombed the bridge. I didn't know what had happened, but the noise sounded like a big bomb. I didn't go down to look at it then because I had a truckload of ice to deliver. I went down later to have a look; it was a heck of a mess. There were many people around; they came from everywhere to see it. Somebody said that the ammunition on the ship went off when that steel fell on it. I don't know, but it was quite an explosion. Everybody thought the Japanese had struck.

Hazel Hessey – Elkton

Something Terrific

I lived in Chesapeake City when the bridge was hit. I was fishing down at the creek. That was Long Creek, which was between our farm on Spear's Hill and the Sisters' farm. I heard this noise and looked towards it and saw that the bridge had been knocked down. It had just disappeared. But I didn't go down there to look. I was just a young guy when it was hit. I heard the sound of a lot of twisting, slamming metal on metal. I knew that something terrific had happened but it didn't occur to me to do something about it. We knew about it within hours, and I guess my father took us all down in the car to see the damage. We saw a lot of twisted metal. The south side went down first and it just pulled everything else down with it.

The thing that struck us, mostly, was that we couldn't get to school at first. They put in a couple of temporary docks - one on the North Side just west of the bridge and the other in the Basin on the South Side. We went to school in a regular boat until they brought the *Gotham* in. But I remember crossing that lift bridge many times. In fact, I recall crossing it hanging behind cars in a sled when there was snow and ice on the road. We did all of those bad things.

You know, before the canal was dug, you could walk from the North Side, where the Presbyterian Church is, all the way over to Bethel. And that's what people used to do. The canal really divided the town in half. Back Creek at one time was called "Bok Creek" after Edward Bok. At one time it was even called "Bok River." Bok was one of the original landowners. He owned Bohemia Manor and most of the territory all the way up to Elkton, I think.

I remember when they brought in the big ferry, the *Gotham*. I watched them build the slips for it. Boy, that was really a trial getting that thing across the canal with that current. A lot of times they couldn't make it and had to turn around and go back. Sometimes the ice held it up, also. But that ferry was kept pretty busy. They used to fill it up quite often going across there. I remember seeing many chicken trucks crossing on it. Big trucks used to haul chickens in crates from the South, the Delmarva Peninsula, I guess. We usually walked on the ferry to get the mail. That was when the post office was on the same block as the Hole in the Wall. I remember going over to the bank on Memorial Day. There was a plaque that was a memorial to the World War I servicemen. The whole school would turn out on Memorial Day. We'd march down there with a little band. We'd stand there and say the Pledge of Allegiance and some people would give speeches.

Paul Spear - Florida

Above the Ericsson Line Boats

When the bridge was struck I was on another bridge, on my way from the Philadelphia Navy Yard to Cape May. I know that they kept the ship there for a while. They couldn't move it because of the weight of the bridge on top of it. But I remember riding up and down on that bridge.

On the way through, heading west - 1938. Photo courtesy of Ester Lupfer

On Saturday nights Ruth and I would go down and ride it up; we always did. We would look down on the Ericsson Line boat which came up from Baltimore and docked at Schaefer's. Later on, though, they banned people from riding on the bridge.

Tweedy Ginn - North Side, near Chesapeake City

Screaming Kids

I was out in the street and I saw the ship run into the lift bridge. I know it really scared my kids; they screamed, you know. It upset me because it was such an awful mess. We lived on the South Side of town, not far from the bridge, and my daughter was just a baby. Oh, it made a racket when it went down. I'd never seen so many people around there in all my life. I remember walking across the old bridge many times. Sometimes I rode a car across, also.

Then the ferries came and we had to ride them. The first ferry was small, and it was kind of scary until I got used to it. Then they brought in the one that we drove the car on. My husband, John, used to pilot that one once in a while, drive it back and forth, you know. They sometimes called him "Captain John." I remember John telling me that one of the pilots was called "Drag Legs." I have no idea why. I remember when Ben Crawford fell into a hole on the ferry. He was walking all around the parked cars when he fell down into the hole that went to the engine room. He hurt himself and there was some trouble about it, but I think they got it straightened out.
Kathryn Hamilton Eveland - North Side

Everything Came Tumbling Down

I was on the bridge the day it was knocked down. I was coming across from the North Side after running an errand for Miss Ida Carter. She sent me to take something over to her daughter. As I walked back across on the bridge, I saw the boat that knocked it down coming around the bend. Then I heard the whistle blow. I've never liked bridges, so when I saw it coming I ran. It's a good thing, because I'd have been stuck if I had been on the other side. I never liked that bridge. I just made it home here before it hit. I was outside when the ship hit. You've never heard such a noise in your life. It was a loud boom, and then I heard all of the piers coming down on the boat.

After that the piers were sticking up out of the water. Later, they had to dynamite them out of there. It was like an earthquake here, the way it shook our foundations. Every time they blew that whistle the ground shook something awful. Now, when the bridge was hit, my sister saw it, and she started screaming. Everything just came tumbling down, and she was standing right beside it. We went down to look at it; it was such a mess. The roadway was on top of the ship and the towers were down in the water.

Lois Maria Sewell - South Side

Like Chains Falling and Rattling

I heard the Lift Bridge fall when the ship hit it. We were living on the Spear Farm at Saint Augustine. I was out in the yard and when that metal fell it sounded like chains falling and rattling. I could usually see the bridge from out there but when I looked toward it that day it wasn't there. So we went in there right away to see what happened. We were about the third car in there. We saw the ship with a lot of the bridge lying on top of it. There weren't many people in there when we arrived.

I remember one time when Charley Butler and I were riding through Chesapeake in his old car. We were going too fast; I know that, and as we approached the bridge the gates came down. We pretty near crashed into those gates. He mashed the brakes down in that old car. It's a wonder we were able to stop. Yeah, we rode across that old bridge a lot of times.

Dan Johnson - Bethel

A Very Weird Noise

I can remember when it happened. I was pregnant at the time and we lived on the North Side of town, on Biddle Street. We lived next to Elsie Loller. I was carrying my son, who was born in February of 1943, so that's the reason I can remember it; the bridge went down in 1942, the summer before. I left the house with Catherine Ann Beaston, Gertrude Sykes, and others. We walked down to the canal and saw where it had been hit, and, of course, the bridge was lying across the ship.

I had a clear view of it because we went in where Archie Crawford's filling station was and walked right down to the edge of the canal. When it was hit I heard a pretty loud noise, even though I was inside the house. It was a very weird noise; I'll tell you. When I went out somebody hollered, "A ship hit the bridge." Then everybody ran down there to see what had happened. I stayed there a while and then walked back home.

Dorothy Hersch - South Side

Missed it by Five Minutes

Oh, sure, I remember when the bridge was struck in Chesapeake City. In fact, Shank Maxwell and I had been in Elkton for some reason, and when we got back the bridge had just been knocked down; the ship had just hit. We missed it by about five minutes. So, naturally, we had to drive all the way around Buck Bridge. But that bridge damage was really something to see. It was a mess. Part of the bridge was on the ship. We used to ride on the bridge when we were kids, especially when there was a carnival in town. That was during the war, and I know that my Uncle Will Purdy ran the small passenger ferry for a while. My cousin, Edgar Rhoades, was the bridge tender on the Lift Bridge there.

Dorsey Johnson - Elkton

Making Hay

I was out in the field on our farm here. We've been here since 1924. I was baling hay at the time and I heard a real loud noise, like a cannon going off. I looked up and saw smoke and dust and then I realized that the bridge was gone and a ship was there, so I stopped baling and got in the car to go down to see what had happened. I stopped at Canal Street, along the canal bank, and saw that the bridge was down and the ship was there. In fact, the bridge was on the ship. The ship's bow was right into the pier on the South Side. They had to get derricks and cranes to lift the steel off the ship; it took a while. Pete Harmer and Cleaver Carter took care of that bridge. They'd climb it to paint it and maintain it.

The steel didn't damage the ship too much because the ship went back on its own power. After that we had to ride the ferry, and I remember driving on it one time when the wind was blowing real hard with a strong tide, and we all ended up almost to Summit Bridge. Of course, it was loaded with cars. They had to get the Corps of Engineer's tug boat to tow it back. It didn't have enough power to fight the tide and wind. The ferry could hold six cars on each side plus trucks and busses in the center.

The *Gotham*, with the north ferry slip at right - circa 1945.
Photo courtesy of Charles Wharton

But as far as the bridge is concerned, I used to ride it up and down many times. The bridge tender used to raise Cain so we would hide behind things so he wouldn't see us.

Ed Loston - North Side

Steel Being Demolished

I was at my home on Cecil Street, playing in the side yard. I heard the sound of steel being demolished. It was loud, but I couldn't see it because of trees and houses in the way. I saw later that the bridge was lying across the ship. I have the feeling that I heard boat whistles but could be wrong. I anticipated our bridge being hit because of the Saint

Georges Bridge being hit earlier. *Nelson Stubbs - North Side*

My Word, Where's the Bridge?

I was six years old and was standing in the grass in my bare feet in front of our farm house on Saint Augustine Road. I had a pile of stones on the ground and I was throwing them - one at a time - at the telephone pole about sixty feet away. I heard a sort of dull clank coming from town. I looked over towards the bridge and saw that it had disappeared. In those days the fields between our farm and the bridge were dotted with small trees, not like the tall, dense ones that now block the view. Back then, I could always see the black lift bridge looming in the distance, outlined against the sky. My grandmother came outside and I pointed and yelled. She said, "My word, where's the bridge?" She then told me, "Not to fret," but to wait till my father came home.

Heading west. Note pulleys at top of bridge tower - circa 1940.
Photo courtesy of Charles Wharton

When he did come home that evening he didn't say much, but the next evening he drove me in town to see what happened. He drove down Bohemia Avenue and turned left on the dirt street that ran between the canal and the Hole-in-the-Wall. He stopped the car just before we got to Mallory Toy's building and we looked out at all of the wreckage. The big ship was where the bridge used to be and the steel was on top of it and in the water. The steel from the bridge was black and all twisted out of shape. I was excited and started jumping around in the car. Pop didn't say much; he let it speak for itself. We didn't get out of the car but just watched it for a while and then drove on back home.

A lady told me recently that she was one of the last persons to go across the bridge before it was destroyed. She said that she had ridden her bicycle across the bridge to the North Side to visit her friend, Hazel Reynolds, who lived in the corner house across from the fire house. On the way across she thought she saw Dr. Davis pass her in his car on his way to the Elkton hospital. She said that she was talking to her friend on the porch when she heard a kind of loud, crumbling sound. She looked around and saw the bridge collapse. It seemed to fall in slow motion, she explained.

She said that her short bike ride left her stranded 14 miles from home. She couldn't ride that far so her friend, Hazel, took her home by way of Summit Bridge. When her husband got home from work, they went back around Summit to the North Side to bring her bike home in the rumble seat of their '29 Nash.

Bob Hazel - South Side, near Chesapeake City

Worried About Our Cousin

We were living in Port Herman when the ship hit the bridge. We came up to see it right after it happened. It was a mess. I don't think we had a phone, but somebody in the neighborhood probably got the news to us. I was about nine, and I remember coming up to see the accident. I was concerned because my Dad's cousin, Edgar Rhoades, had just gotten off duty when it happened. He operated the lift bridge, but, of course, at that time the little operator's house was on land, not up on the bridge as it used to be.

Audrey Johnson McDonough – Earlville

My God, They've hit the Bridge

Ralph and I had gone over town to the post office and when we came back the bridge had started up, but we knew the bridge tender, George Knott, so he lowered it to let us go across. And by the time we got home, that ship had struck the bridge. George was not in the little house on the bridge. They had built one on land on the South Side. But I did see the ship coming as we crossed over the bridge. I didn't think anything of it; it was just another ship coming through.

We drove on home and had just gotten out of the car. We lived on the North Side, on the corner of Hemphill and Cecil, across from the Lake house. Anyway, when we got out of the car – Oh, my gosh - we heard a crash and my brother, Reedy, happened to be sitting on the porch at the time; he said, "My God, they've hit the bridge." So we all ran down by Schaefer's and looked at it from there. They say that guns went off, but we didn't hear any, unless they went off at the same time as the loud crash. The concrete and steel was all twisted and lying on the ship. The worker threw those guns up in the air so they wouldn't go off and hit anybody. But when we ran down there they wouldn't let you get too close.

I really wish that my brother, Reedy Benson, was still alive. He could really tell about it. He was an encyclopedia about it. But I wish I could remember more; you know, you're in a state of shock when something like that happens. It came down a few minutes after we crossed over it. But I remember when I used to ride it when it went up. I did it all the time; I loved it. You could look all over town. Ralph rode it too, but when Saint Georges went down they wouldn't let you; they put guards on it.

Eleanor Northrop - North Side

Not My Sweet Potato!

Why, I certainly have a vivid memory of the day our bridge was hit. Mother was hanging up clothes that day and I was supposed to have been cleaning up the dishes, and I just heard this awful racket. But, being a kid, I didn't pay much attention to it. I was doing something wrong at the time. I was in the corner of the kitchen eating a raw sweet potato, which I knew I shouldn't have been doing because the doctor told mother that it wasn't good for me. All of a sudden I heard all this racket. Mother was yelling and screaming and I thought, "Oh, I've had it." Then she came in to check on me and that's when I heard everyone yelling that the Japs were bombing us and that our bridge was being bombed. People were crying and neighbors who had been mad at each other were hugging and carrying on something terrible. And I thought, "My gosh, they're not worried about me and my sweet potato."

That's about all I remember, except for the noise of the ship hitting the bridge. It was just like a heavy roar, like a clack of thunder, something like that. I wasn't allowed to go down and look at it; my life was very protected. Being a girl, I wasn't allowed to do any of the good stuff. But I remember walking that bridge to go to school. I was the only girl with a whole bunch of boys. The Reynolds boys, the Sheldons, and the Dolors would meet with my brothers and we'd all go across that bridge. I remember when one of the army guards ran and got a big bow the wind had blown off my hair. He was guarding the bridge and that made me feel pretty important.

Becky Caleb May – Elkton

A Terrible Mess

I was on the North Side, swimming in the canal with John Thornton and some other kids. We were down the bank from where Bayard Bedwell lived. I heard a loud crash. Then I saw that the bridge wasn't there. We went down later and saw a terrible mess.

John Dolor - North Side

Money Worries

I was on the side porch of our house on Biddle Street. I was nine years old and with my uncle who was recuperating from an appendix operation. I heard a crash that carried on for several seconds. I didn't know what it was at first but thought the end of the world was here. I think I heard shots - maybe shells exploding - but it may have been the two towers crashing down. I went around front but couldn't see what happened because of trees and buildings in the way. When I finally went down there I saw the mess - the steel from the bridge all over the ship. Military men were keeping people away and keeping them from taking pictures. The soldiers were staying on the North Side.

    I remember being worried about how I would get the money I had saved out of the bank. The bank was on the South Side of course. The government patrol boat was first used to take people back and forth, then the small ferries, and finally the big car ferry. We kids used to play on the bulldozers and other machinery that were used to build the ferry slips. We would jump on them and pretend to operate them at the end of the day when the workers left. I recall getting to school three different ways: walking over the old lift bridge, riding the ferries, and walking over the new bridge before it was finished. Paul Benson and I walked across that unfinished bridge a lot.

    I remember how Dr. Davis used to have a car on both sides of the canal, near the ferry, so he could get to his patients quicker. One time I was not able to get home from school for a while because a man had jumped off of the old Wilson Line boat to commit suicide. He just handed his wife his wallet and jumped. They put the Wilson Line steamer in the North Side ferry slip while they tried to find his body.

I remember also the loud booming sound when they dynamited the concrete abutments out of there. The whistle would blow and then time would pass before the explosion. I got so I could time it perfectly. This was some years later, well after the bridge went down. It had to be done so they could widen the canal.

Merritt Collins, Sr. - New Castle, Delaware

The Long Jump

When that bridge was hit two of my relatives had just died. When we took them to the Bethel Cemetery we had to go all the way around Summit to come in. I came back later to see the damage caused by the ship. The bridge was lying across the bow. I was just getting ready to go in the service.

I remember riding on that old bridge. I jumped off of it one time when it was twenty feet in the air. Earl Sykes was the operator and Nola Knotts' husband was the superintendent, and he came out and picked me up off of the sidewalk - thought I was dead. The bridge was still moving when I jumped off at twenty feet. I didn't jump in the water; I jumped on the road bed. We used to have fights up at the school, and Earl Harmer was running after me to beat me up, so as the bridge was going up I got on it and jumped off the other side. But, yes, we used to ride it a lot.

My wife's brother used to climb it every night, clear up to the top and sit on top of the tower. I used to ride up with Earl Sykes and get in the bridge house and ride up with him. We could look right down at the ships passing, right into the smoke stack. They had gates years ago that used to stop the traffic. I could see the boats coming and get ready. They had the army engineer boats and pilot boats moving through all of the time and had to lift it for them often.

David Bedwell - South Side, near Chesapeake City

Chaos Everywhere

We had gone shopping in Elkton and when we came down Lock Street we saw all of the activity. I wasn't too old, about ten, and Mr. Earl Sykes was driving the car. We went down to look and there were many people and a lot of excitement, a lot of commotion going on. Everyone was gawking; you know how it is when a tragedy happens, everybody talking at once. I remember the crowd of people being there but that's about all. I saw that the bridge wasn't there; it was on the ship. There was chaos everywhere. I remember going down and saying, "What in the world happened?"

Marjorie Austin - North Side

Milking the Cows

Well, I was milking the cows on our farm near South Chesapeake. Our small farm was located about where the Motor Vehicle building is now. I was fourteen years old. I heard a crash, a lot like the sound of cars colliding. I looked towards the sound and saw that the bridge towers weren't there, so I rode my bike down there as close as I could and saw the ship with part of the bridge on the bow.

There were soldiers guarding the bridge at the time, and they didn't want people taking pictures so they were taking their cameras. Also, the soldiers were upset because they were on the South Side and their base of operations was on the North Side; they weren't quite sure what to do because there was no way over there. I watched for a while and then rode on back home.

Pete Terreszcuk - North Side

There Goes Your Bridge, Brownie!

I was upstairs in bed, here in our house on Saint Augustine Road. I think I must have been sick that morning. Mother was working at Schaefer's Restaurant, and Daddy was there with her at the time. You know he used to work for the government, and he had gone to Schaefer's for lunch that day. Mother happened to be looking out the screen door on the side of the restaurant, and after a while she said, "There goes your bridge, Brownie; come quick!" and before he got over there, it was over. She saw the towers weaving back and forth. She said that one fell into the field on the North Side, and, of course, the bridge was guarded then, and the guards used to sleep in the little house by the bridge on the North Side. I think they built the house specifically for them to live in.

Link from the lift bridge chain, note penny on top. Photographed by the author.

Well, when the bridge was struck, they went flying across that field, and one of them stopped running; he couldn't move because one of the links in the chain fell right behind him. He wasn't hit or anything, but he was in shock. The chain moved the bridge span up and down. Each link weighed at least a hundred pounds and he just missed being hit by it.

But I didn't hear anything when the bridge was hit because I was in bed asleep. I didn't find out about it from my parents because they couldn't get home; they had to drive around. It wasn't a short drive any longer. I first heard about it from Esther Luzetsky; she lived at the Hole-In-The-Wall then, and she probably called me. What a surprise! Mother came home later that day but Daddy had to stay on that ship, the *Franz Klasen*; he was on call 24 hours a day. For a while they thought destroying the bridge was sabotage; it was war-time, of course.

As a young girl I used to ride up and down on the bridge many times. Every time we heard a ship blow three times, Ester and I would run to the bridge. We had time because we were alerted. Of course, she lived at the Hole-In-The-Wall and I lived just up the street, next to the bank. The bridge operator worked in a little shack that was high up; they had to climb a ladder to get up to it. A lot of times they just couldn't see us underneath. We were on this side and they were distracted by the boat and didn't see us. But the operators knew us, so that's why they didn't say anything either. Mr. Sykes was one of them, I know. That bridge span rising and falling didn't make much noise, except for the chains creaking, and that was it.

Sometimes the Ericsson Line boats would come through. As a young girl I remember sailing on one of them one time. Mother and Daddy took Franny and me up to Philadelphia and back. I recall that when we were eating dinner the waitress put finger bowls on the table. Mother looked at me and said, "Anna, don't you dare play in that." And I must have said, "Why?" because then she said, "That's to wash your fingers."

Anna Brown Williams - South Side

Cover of pamphlet advertising the Ericsson Line. Courtesy of Walter Cooling.

Jingling Bells

I was living on Canal Street when it happened, and I remember hearing everything, a lot of noise. It sounded like bells, jingling and jingling when the bridge fell down. That's all the sound I heard; it happened so quickly. I was inside my home when it happened, but the noise made us all run out on Canal street, right down in front of the house. Then we walked down to see what was going on. There were a lot of people there. I saw the boat with the bridge on top of it, the part that went up was lying across it.

Clara Wharton - South Side

Snapping Sticks

I was on the back porch of our house, next to the store on Biddle Street. I heard it when it went down. From that distance it sounded like sticks breaking that you put in your hands. You know what we did as kids? We'd get a bunch of sticks and twist them until they snapped to see if we could break them all. It was a crash; my mother came running and fell over us because she thought that somebody had dropped a bomb. It was a horrible sound. My recollection of it was hearing a snapping, crackling sound, and it wasn't just the one boom and it was over; it was slow - not real slow - but it took several seconds to go down and position itself on the ship.

I went right down there with Edgar Pensel, and at that time they had the guards on both ends of the bridge, and they confiscated the film of anybody who went up to take pictures. They didn't take the cameras but they'd take the film out. But, yes, when we arrived the bridge was down and the fire whistle blew and the engines went out. Everybody knew it was down, of course, because you couldn't see the towers; they were gone!

It didn't take long, though, to get a boat to transport kids to school. At first they used one of the Corps of Engineers' boats, the *Pilot*, I think. Then they built the foot ferry, one that held fifteen people. Next they used a bigger boat, the *Victory*, which held twenty three. They weren't too long getting the big ferry in, the *Gotham*. They were less than three months getting the ferry slips and the approach roads built. Well, they had to move fast because the post office was on the South Side, and back then there was no mail delivery. And, of course, the school was over there.

We all didn't seem too excited at the time. The excitement came when we tried to figure out how we were going to get to school - what we were going to do, because at that time I walked across the bridge from my father's store to the elementary school. Something I remember, by the way, is how they had huge cement blocks on the ends of the bridge, because if it snowed they had to counterbalance it so it would go up and down. We used to run to get on the bridge to ride it up, and the tenders were right on it at the time.

Lewis Collins - North Side

Shrimp Boat

I was at home, on Canal Street, and I remember that when the bridge was down they had army guards all around. They wouldn't let us mess around down there because at that time there was a war going on, and the ship that hit the bridge was German. I remember the old ferry that took us across to school. Ed Sheridan was the captain and he was a good friend of my dad's. Many times I would ride up there with my dad and Captain Sheridan. Sometimes Ed would have a big pot of shrimp, and we'd ride back and forth eating shrimp. But I do remember when they dynamited those bridge piers out of there, but I didn't think much of it at that age.

Bayard Bedwell - North Side

Strange Homecoming

I was working in Wilmington when the bridge went down. I think my wife called me to tell me that the bridge had been hit and that she was many miles from home. But come to think of it, I had come home before I found out about it. I probably came to the North Side because I was carrying Iler Lum and Frank Filligame back and forth. They worked at Jackson and Sharp's up there and I worked at Hollingsworth's, which was located about where the museum and ball field are now.

Did I ever ride on that old bridge? Darn right I did. Other people used to stand up there and ride too. I think that the little control house on the bridge was made of steel plates.

I also remember riding from here to Baltimore on the *Lord Baltimore*. I went with my mother; we boarded just below the Pivot Bridge, near the Pumping Station, at the Ericsson Line Wharf. It was on the North Side, near the Hollow. But sometimes we boarded at the locks. I recall how much smoke they put out, and how narrow they were - about 20 feet wide. If few were going down at night we'd get on in the evening at 8 or 9 o'clock. We'd get into Baltimore about midnight. It took three or four hours, depending on the tide and the wind. That was in the early twenties; I was about ten years old.

When we pulled into Baltimore my mother and I would walk out onto Light Street and catch a trolley down to South Baltimore to see my aunts. We stayed about a week, and caught another steamer back to Chesapeake City. The boats generally stopped at Town Point, Betterton, and sometimes Rambo's Wharf, which was where White Crystal is now.

John Sager - South Side

Outrunning the Nuns

I know exactly where I was when the bridge was hit. We were at the hall on Basil Avenue having catechism classes with the nuns. I don't know how it happened; it's been so long, but somebody said, "A ship hit the bridge and knocked it down." When we kids heard that we took off running as fast as we could towards Chesapeake, and the nuns ran after us, trying to stop us. But we kept on going into Chesapeake and, sure enough, there was the ship with the bridge lying on top of it.

It really looked bad, mangled and just across the top of the ship, a heck of a looking mess, really. I was pretty young at the time but I remember it was terrible looking. We were inside so we didn't hear anything, but it's a wonder we didn't because of all that structure coming down, all of that metal. We ran all the way to where the stop sign and barricade are now, pretty close.

Somebody said that the ship had a German pilot and that he rammed it intentionally, but we didn't know if that was true or not. But the funny thing that I remember was hearing the nuns calling, "Come back, come back," and the way they were after us. We were all yelling and laughing and running as fast as we could. We would not have known about the bridge if someone hadn't come in and told us - a big mistake. We flew, and that ended the classes for that day. We weren't about to go back. After a while I just walked on back home.

I remember riding that ferry a lot when it was there. One time I was riding my bike to get on the ferry, down the hill on the North Side, and I was going fast so I could catch it, and my chain came off. With no brakes I went sailing onto the ferry and crashed into a guy's bumper. I didn't damage the car but the owner was really upset.

Mike Yonko - South Side

An Airplane Dropping Bombs

I was scrubbing my front porch at the time. We lived on Cecil Street, the house next to Wilfong's. Tweedy Ginn used to live there. I heard a very loud noise, like the bridge was being bombed. It was such an explosion that I thought a plane had bombed the bridge. My husband was a truck driver for Wooleyhan's, and he was driving down Sisters' Hill when he saw the bridge go down.

I'll never forget it; he walked up our front porch and said, "I was coming down the road looking at the bridge and the first thing I knew I didn't see it; it was gone." When he said that I was kind of scared. I just stood there with the garden hose in my hand. But once I found out that it wasn't an airplane dropping bombs, I walked down to look. I noticed how all of the traffic was piled up there - trucks and cars lined up. I thought the ship was practically under water because of all of the weight. Oh, what we had to go through - getting to the other side. Of course, the bank, post office, stores, and many things were on the South Side. I recall how many people - sightseers and others - came to Chesapeake City that day. My husband had to help his father run the store; it was so busy. He had to dip ice cream for a long time. They were so busy that they couldn't put the lids back on the containers. They held two and a half gallons, and he dipped until they ran out of ice cream. When he came home he said that both wrists were sore from so much scooping.

Not much room to spare between the towers of Reedy Point Bridge - circa 1969

    I still remember how bad the noise was when they blasted the cement abutments out so they could widen the canal. The whistles would blow and then the dynamite would go off. It was awful; the windows shook and the blast cracked the chimneys.

I used to ride up on that bridge, but one time I started to walk over, pushing Jimmy, our son, in the baby coach. All at once the bridge started to go up, so I had to pull the coach back in a hurry. I used to watch my sister, Madeline, dive off the bridge. She used to dive towards the little white control house, but far enough over so she wouldn't hit anything. Now, a lot earlier than that I used to walk across the locks to school sometimes. Once, when they let the water in, it really scared me. I was afraid I'd fall in.

I still remember when the steamers stopped at the Ericsson Line Building to load and unload freight and a few passengers. I remember when they closed the locks. I used to swim down there. I never rode the boats, but in the evenings I used to go down there and watch them. The smoke used to just pour out of them.

Edna Gorman - North Side

Dopey Dreams

I had just come out of swimming, and was climbing up the bank down in front of Eddie Taylor's. That's where we always changed into our bathing suits in the high grass. I was climbing up when I heard an awful noise, like somebody had dropped a load of metal, a long clatter. Then somebody yelled, "The bridge fell down," so everybody ran down there to see. I heard a lot of boat whistles blowing just before the noise. I ran down Canal Street to the Hollow to look, and it looked kind of bare; the span was draped across the ship. I'm pretty sure the ship had tugs on it because after Saint Georges they were mandatory.

I remember one time before the bridge was destroyed, when I was on the South Side swimming from the wharf over to the point - back and forth - when a ship came through with a tug boat on the front and on the side, and this particular ship almost took the bridge down, because it glanced off the pilings. The lead tug had a guy out there with an ax trying to chop the hawser off to keep the tug from flipping over. There was a series of pilings which had long, heavy planks attached to protect the bridge. The vessels would slide along the planking instead of getting hung up in the pilings.

Well, this ship grazed the pilings, just bounced right off of them because the bow had been up past the bridge and it just bounced off after that tug boat cut that line off. He was blowing her whistle while the guy swung that ax; the tug almost swamped. It was leaning over so far that I don't know how the guy could have stood up to cut the hawser off. It was the South Side, just like the ship that finally took the bridge down. If the tide was coming towards the ship when it's headed west, it just forced it into the south end of the bridge. The way the canal was then, the tide would bounce off the shore and then bounce towards the bridge, so there was a natural force towards that south tower.

But when I went down there a couple of days later, people were picking up souvenirs, whatever they could pick up. At one time I had a half a link of chain from the bridge. It was a long time before they blasted those abutments out of there - not until they widened the canal in the sixties. When the bridge was hit a lot of people wondered if anybody was on it when it went down, because we used to ride up and down on it just for fun, especially in the summertime when we were off school. I rode on it a few times but I didn't like it. I don't like heights.

I've been on it when it was ready to go up and I had to jump off. Sometimes, if you were in the middle of it, you had to run and jump to get off it. They didn't wait for you to get off. If you were there you went up. I still have dreams about that bridge. In the dreams, I'm going across it and there are parts missing; sometimes there are no hand railings on it. I have all kinds of dopey dreams about that old bridge.

Walter "Buddy" Carlton - Newark, Delaware

Surprise!

I was in the service. I found out about it when I came home from Fort Meade. The ferry was in operation then. I was going with my wife at the time and she told me. Other people told me about it also.

Butch Eveland lived just up the street and also Jack Titter was in Chesapeake City when it was hit. They told me about it years afterwards. Evidently Butch saw it happen.

Ralph Watson - North Side, near Chesapeake City

Folded Like an Accordion

I was swimming off of the dock, right where the Canal Creamery is now. I watched the ship hit the bridge and watched it fall. I saw the ship coming and heard the whistles blowing. At that time the canal was so narrow, about 250 feet and crooked, and each ship that went through had two tugs on it to assist it, one on the bow and one on the stern. With this ship, the tug on the bow stayed right with it when it went into a sheer, and it was going to pin the tug between the bridge and the ship. I remember seeing the guys cutting the hawsers with axes to clear the tug. She hit the tower on the South Side, and the tower folded like an accordion and went down on the bow of the ship. The main span was up in the air, and the other tower went kind of back towards the north roadway, Lock Street. Then the lift or span kind of turned a little bit.

Swimming at the Burnt House – Bobby Hazel is about to jump from the channel marker. Note unfinished over-head bridge at right – circa 1948. Photo courtesy of Tom Newlin.

They stopped traffic about where Tommy Vaughn's bed and breakfast is now, and on the other side they stopped traffic at the intersection of Lock and Bank streets, probably where Mrs. Kitty Maloney lived. They kept the cars back that far because some parts of the bridge landed in the street. The ship had a deck gun, which went off. I'm not sure, but I think a man on the bow - on watch - was badly injured. He either jumped off or stuff fell on him. Within forty-five minutes to an hour, the canal banks were lined with soldiers from Aberdeen, because she was a German tanker with a German crew and she had been captured, so they posted the soldiers along the canal on both sides to make sure none of them got off the ship. Of course, we kids tried to swim out there but they kept us away from it.

I was ten years old. We used to swim off the dock all the time. We used a diving board that Bob Miller gave us. But when that bridge was hit it sounded like rumbling thunder. There were fire and sparks and dust flying everywhere. It just reminded me of thunder. I watched and at first I thought it would miss the bridge. Of course, the bridge was very narrow where you went through; they had a fender system, and the northwest wind was a factor. One of the tugs on the ship was the *Falk* and the company that owned her was Curtis Bay Towing. The *Falk* stood out because she was silver and fairly new and had a fancy, solid guard rail around the front of her. The tugs couldn't help the ship because once she took that sheer she went right on in there.

My first thought was "How's my dad going to get home tonight?" After they cleared the ship and the bridge away, and got the canal opened, we went down there on low tide and found pieces of links out of the big chains that were on the counterweights. We got a lot of money from the scrap man who used to come down from Wilmington every Saturday. We didn't keep a thing, though.

But getting back to the sound of the collision, it was like thunder; you know, the weight falling on the bow of that ship, which was probably hollow, would be like hitting on a drum. There was a lot of grinding and sparks flying and dust in the air, and it seemed almost like slow motion; it didn't give up too easily, that old bridge. I guess the ship just took the heart out of it and it had to come down, but it sure seemed like slow motion. Then the small passenger ferry was here. That's when they built the docks for the car ferry and also Ferry Slip Road.

Clifton Beck - North Side

Canal Street Commandos

I was playing on the canal bank by Bedwell's with a bunch of kids. We were the Canal Street Commandos. We used to call the area "Clay Point" because there was nothing but clay down there.

Flyer advertising the Rio Theater. The Rio was on the South Side, next to B.F. Nichols Shoe Repairing - circa 1942. Courtesy of Ester Luzetsky.

We used to go down and cover ourselves up with clay and then jump in the water. We'd also slide down that bank on pieces of cardboard. I didn't pay any attention to the ships going by. We were too busy having fun to notice.

I was six at the time, and I remember traveling back and forth on the ferry. But the first thing I remember hearing was a bunch of noise. Then everybody ran down there to where the apartments were in the Hollow to look. When we got there I remember all of the people there looking at the mess, and I saw that the bridge wasn't there. But all we kids cared about was how we were going to get over town to see the Saturday afternoon movies at the Rio.

Charles Wharton - South Side

Clattering Lumber

I was home on Biddle Street at the time, and by the time I got to Canal Street everybody was hollering, "The bridge went down." Everybody was moving down Biddle Street. I was outside when it hit and it sounded like something being unloaded with a continuous rattle. I had heard the lumber company dump lumber before, when the flatbed trucks used to pull out from underneath a load of lumber, and the lumber would clatter, clatter as it dropped from the truck to the ground, except the sound came from way down the street where it was hit and I didn't know that that sound was the bridge until I got out front and somebody started hollering. Then I ran down to the bridge with everybody else.

I went down Biddle Street to about the Presbyterian Church. There was an empty field there then, so I could see the ship. It was an amazing sight. Nobody seemed overly excited. We were just thinking: "What will we do now?" It was so funny not to see the bridge standing up in the air; it had always been there. With the old bridge it was nothing to leave one side of town for the other. It was so easy to just walk across to Postell's soda fountain on the corner. When it went down it changed the whole town.

Nancy Carlton - Newark, Delaware

Ba*loom*!

I was swimming in the canal, opposite our family home on Biddle Street Extension. My brother, Tots, was probably with us. I think we may have been skinny-dipping. I was about twelve years old. At that time there was lots of action on the canal. Many naval vessels especially - LSTS, PT boats, and others. The canal was constantly busy - heavy traffic. We kids loved the PT boats because they produced huge waves for us to ride. I watched a tanker go by and a few minutes later heard a loud clunk, a big thud; it went ba*loom*. I could tell it was metal on metal.

We all ran down Canal Street and saw a maze of people on both sides of the canal. They were all worried that there may have been people on the bridge when it was hit. I used to ride up and down on the bridge lots of times. The cables would shake as it rose and fell - a real thrill for us kids. My dad, Frank Sheldon, worked there and would let us ride, but most other kids weren't allowed. But that day we saw the destruction. There was steel all crisscrossed on the ship's bow. The concrete counterweights had crashed into the water.

Roland "Flint" Sheldon - North Side

Above The Yachts

I was working at Aberdeen Proving Grounds when the bridge was knocked down. Somebody at work told me that it was down; news about it spread pretty fast. A carload of us went down to look at it, and we were surprised to see the bridge lying across the deck of the ship. We had to go around Summit to get home. But it didn't take long to get a little ferry to take people across. Sometimes I'd leave my car on the South Side, ride the ferry, and ride to work with somebody who lived on the North Side.

I used to ride up on that old bridge a lot in the summertime; lots of people did. It was up and down a good bit in those days. There was lots of traffic - yachts and government vessels. The bridge tenders would let us kids ride. They didn't care. We liked to look right down on those big yachts as they went under.

Dick Titter - South Side, near Chesapeake City

The Extra Bike Ride

I had been to the store for my mother at Tatman's, next to the American Store on the South Side. I had ridden back over the bridge and had just pulled in to our house here on Biddle Street. I saw the ship as I was riding by. It was blowing out here as it went by, before the curve, just east of the pumping station. I got home and had just walked in the house. My mother had picked some beans from the garden and she was fixing them when we heard this noise. She jumped at the unusual sound. My father was in bed from his car accident. He had been in Saint Georges when its bridge went down, and he said, "Wait a minute," and we heard the other tower fall, and he said, "The ship knocked that bridge down."

My mom was all upset because my brother worked at Schaefer's, right next to the bridge. So she made me go back in town and told me not to fool around. We had just moved out there and during the war you couldn't get a phone right away. When I went in, I found out that the bridge had fallen in the canal, so I hopped on my bike and came back and told my mother. Then I looked out in the canal and saw four or five ships out there. They turned them around up there by Bethel.

But when all that metal fell in it made a boom, as you might imagine. When I went down I could see guns on the ship. The one on the bow was standing straight up. I guess that was from the jolt of the collision. I saw that the bridge part that rose up and down had fallen right across the bow and the towers fell in the water, not on the shore. The big thing that I remember was that I was one of the last ones to cross the bridge, because I was on my bike, and by the time I got home it was down. I heard the sound when I got home, which was just beyond Sheldon's. You could hear it well out there; it was noisy, a big booming sound. The ship hit the South Side of the bridge when it took a sheer and rammed. And when we lived here, before they widened the canal, we could hear the ships run aground once in a while. We'd hear them crunching when they hit.

But I used to ride up and down on the old bridge. I can tell you now because Dad's not around. You could see all over up there. That's the highest spot around. The old Ericsson Line boats used to come through and they'd have to raise the bridge high for those things. That was before the ships started coming through. I remember the steamer, *John Cadwalader*. My grandmother and aunts used to come up from Baltimore on those steamboats. They'd get off at Schaefer's in the morning to visit us, and then get back on board in the evening to return. I never rode the boats, but I used to ride up on the old

Lift Bridge and look down on them as they passed under. That was in 1934 or 1935.

But I'll never forget the bridge being hit, because the ships used to have to blow right about here somewhere for the bridge. It blew three blasts of the whistle, and the bridge tender lowered the gates. But when I heard the whistles from the ship that hit, I was just coming across on my bike. I know that I headed fast up the street because I wanted to get home, and then I had to go back. Those three blasts were the last they'd have to make.

John Reynolds - North Side

The Bridge was Gone

I was at the Swyka home on Saint Augustine Road, and Nick's mother and I were washing clothes. We were out in the yard where the pump was and I was pumping the water while she was rinsing the clothes. We heard this noise and we looked up and the bridge was gone. It made a real loud sound when it fell, a big boom. We looked up and couldn't figure out what was the matter. Then we realized that our bridge had fallen down. It was exciting. Later, when Nick and I went to town, we saw that a ship had hit the bridge and some parts of the metal bridge were lying across the ship.

Mildred Swyka – South Side, near Summit, Delaware

Author's Note: The next recollection concerns the destruction of the Saint Georges Bridge by a freighter in 1939. Donald Michael knew exactly where he was when it happened.

I Felt the Jolt

As I recall, it was around New Years in 1939 when I was on the freighter, *Waukegan,* when it knocked down the Saint Georges Bridge. It was in the morning, probably about eight or nine o'clock. There's not much to tell; the ship started blowing the whistle when it went out of control, for the bridge tender I assume. Then the ship swung over and hit the North Side of the bridge. There was a pretty strong current and it just sheered into it. The *Waukegan* was my first ship.

I was a mess boy on there. I was not on deck at the time, but was cleaning up the dishes. I was a little more than midway towards the stern, and I knew that we were in trouble once the whistle started blowing. Everybody knew then because the general alarm went off about the same time, and all of the men went to their stations. The general alarm was a very shrill bell.

The grounded *Waukegan* after hitting the Saint Georges Bridge - east view.

I was sixteen years old. We were coming from England, Hamburg, and I think we stopped at New York and Philadelphia to take off cargo. We were headed for Baltimore, and, of course, that collision ended the ship's career. The bow had a pretty big hole in it, above the water line, and they took it down to Baltimore. The engines were good so they took it to England during the war, sank it, and used it as a breakwater.

I was on her last voyage, and when you're young there's nothing like your first ship. I caught it out of Baltimore, and I think we made three trips. When it hit the bridge the steering engine was bad, and just at the time, when the ship got to the bridge, the steering engine malfunctioned. The man at the wheel couldn't do anything, and the pilot was telling him what to do, how to steer it, but it wouldn't answer the rudder;

that's the whole thing. The day before, we were in Delaware City when the steering first went out. The guy who was on the wheel couldn't steer it, so the chief engineer worked on the steering engine - it was in the stern - and tried to correct the problem, but then the next day the collision happened.

Baltimore was the *Waukegan's* port of call. The company was the old Oriole Line, if I recall correctly. I remember that I was at sea when the Chesapeake City Bridge was hit. I'd have to check my discharge records to tell exactly. But that was some day for me, when the *Waukegan* hit; it was after Christmas and I was coming back from Europe. I was inside and didn't know what they were blowing for. It could have been for a small boat that they had hit, but I never dreamed that it had hit a bridge. Anybody who was sleeping, off watch, or in the engine room wouldn't know what was hit until they came out on deck.

Collision at Saint Georges, Delaware - Many came to see the damage

16-year-old Donald Michael on the *Waukegan*. Photo courtesy of Mr. Michael.

I had a camera and took some pictures, although they didn't want anybody to take them, saying they would confiscate the film. I didn't know what was going on when I came up on deck; I was new. All of the deck hands wanted to get to the bow to see what the problem was. Of course, everybody felt the jolt when it hit. As I said, it was right after breakfast time and I was cleaning up. I rode the ship down to Baltimore till they decided what to do with it. But it took a day or two until they sent a tug from the Curtis Bay Towing Company to tow it down. There was nothing wrong with the ship's engine, but it was that steering engine that was bad and they wouldn't let us move the ship because if that steering engine malfunctioned once it would do it again and maybe hit something else.

So we got out of the canal with the assistance of tugs. They took it to a pier to unload the rest of the cargo, and then they took it to the shipyard. They paid the crew off and then I don't know what happened to it then. I was transferred to the *Liberty,* the same type of ship and the same company. The ship was built in Carney, New Jersey, I believe. They were World War I types of ships. At that time Hitler was getting pretty bad and a lot of people were shipping their furniture and things out of places like Hamburg to the Atlantic Seaboard, to somewhere along the United States.

The rest of the cargo at that time was Peat Moss - very light - and that's what made it bad because those ships in the North Atlantic, having such light cargo as furniture and peat moss, were always rolling and pitching. They would store the cargo in three different decks below the main deck. Also, all of those ships had tanks full of sea water, which served as a ballast to load them down to keep them from rolling so much in bad weather.

Looking back, I can tell you that nobody on the *Waukegan* did any running to the stern; nobody was frightened the way they were when that tanker hit the

Chesapeake City Bridge. You see, that tanker's cargo may have been highly flammable - oil or aviation fuel maybe - and that's why they ran aft; that would scatter anybody. The *Waukegan* didn't have tugs attending her the way the *Franz Klasen* did. I don't know why she had those tugs on her.

    I was on freighters all during the Second World War, sailing across the Atlantic and so forth, when the Germans were blowing up ships from their submarines. I've been lucky. I made a trip on the *S.S. Paul Hamilton* and then got off of it. The very next trip it was bombed, and since it was carrying explosives the whole thing just disintegrated. It had 8000 tons of ammo aboard. 504 troops were killed that day. I got off at the right time. It was one month to the day after I was discharged from it.

    Then I was on another ship, the *S.S. Solon Tulman,* and got off of it six months before the Japanese bombed Pearl Harbor. The ship was torpedoed off Balboa shortly after I got off of it. We had gone all over the Pacific: the Philippines, Australia, China, Japan, and other countries.

                  Donald Michael - North Side

Donald Michael remembers that day in 1939. Photographed in December, 1999.

Afterthoughts

This collection dealt mainly with people who were in or near Chesapeake City when the bridge was hit, those who experienced the collision and its aftermath. Some of the accounts given here, however, were second-hand, from residents who were in the service or had business away from town that morning in July. Their reactions - based on what relatives and friends told them - are valid nonetheless.

So many people have died since 1942 though, taking their unique impressions with them. For many of them, however, friends and relatives have remembered their descriptions and supplied them for this compilation. Over 57 years have passed since the bridge was hit, but practically everyone who was kind enough to share their impressions, remembered the events as if they occurred yesterday, and if we're lucky, their recollections, preserved here, will last much more than another 57 years, well into the next millennium.

A majestic sight, the Chesapeake City lift bridge - west view - circa 1939. Photo from an undated post card, courtesy of Buddy Carlton

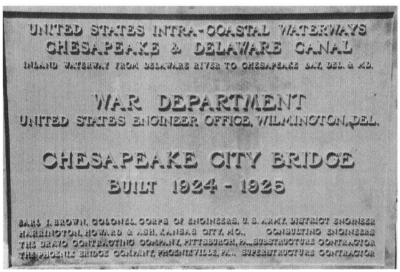

Tablet that was once displayed by the Corps of Engineers at the south approach to the bridge. Photo provided by the Corps of engineers

Southeast view of the lift bridge - circa 1926, couresty of Morrison Watson.

A 1929 aerial view, with Long Bridge at left and the remains of the lock

An aerial view, with part of the Causeway - west view - circa 1935

Reflection – Circa 1940

About the Author

Robert Hazel is a fifth-generation resident of the Chesapeake City area. He lives with his wife on the land once farmed by his great, great grandfather, William Hudson, who died in 1851. Before the Civil War, Thomas Parker Hazel, another great, great grandfather, was a merchant and postmaster in the community of Saint Augustine. Hazel's great grandfather, Jacob Truss, was a tugboat captain who talked about seeing Civil War battles in the distance as he piloted his boat on the Potomac River. A graduate of the University of Delaware and West Chester University, Robert Hazel has written several books about historic Chesapeake City, Maryland.

List of those who remembered the accident

Austin, Marjorie
Battersby, Birdie
Beck, Clifton
Bedwell, Bayard
Bedwell, David
Biddle, Dave
Biggs, Dwayne
Blendy, Barbara
Blevins, Audrey
Breza, Charles
Breza, Mamie
Breza, Paul
Briscoe, Bill
Bristow, Betty
Brown, Anna
Brown, Francis
Carlton, Buddy
Carlton, Nancy
Chicosky, Emil
Clark, Albert
Collins, Lewis
Collins, Merritt
Conley, John
Cooling, Walter
Crawford, Helen
Davis, Eloise
DiGirolamo, Al
Dolor, John
Elwood, Frank
Eveland, Gertrude
Eveland, John, Jr.
Eveland, Kathryn
Farlow, Doris
Foard, Thomas
Ginn, Clifton
Ginn, Ruth
Ginn, Tweedy
Givens, Emily

Gleason, Alma
Gorman, Edna
Hazel, Bob
Hazel, Dolores
Hersch, Dorothy
Hessey, Hazel
Hotra, Joe
Johnson, Dan
Johnson, Dorsey
Johnson, Richard
Johnston, Snake
Kelly, Norma
King, Thelma
Kruger, Margaret
Lake, Ted
Lee, Frances
Lee, Harold
Loston, Ed
Lum, Jack
Lumpkin, Claude
Luzetsky, Alex
Luzetsky, Esther
Luzetsky, John
Luzetsky, Nicky
May, Becky
McDonough, Audrey
McNeal, Gertrude
Michael, Donald
Miklas, Jeanette
Morgan, Evelyn
Newlin, Tom
Nichols, Bob
Northrop, Eleanor
Northrop, Ralph
Ohrel, Miriam
Purner, Allen
Reynolds, John
Rhoades, Freddy

Sager, John
Savin, Ellen
Savin, Joe, Jr.
Schrader, Anna
Schrader, Earl
Sewell, Lois
Sheldon, Flint
Sheldon, Tots
Sheridan, Dick
Spear, Paul
Stubbs, Dorothy
Stubbs, Eddie
Stubbs, Grason
Stubbs, Jimmy
Stubbs, Madeline
Stubbs, Nelson
Sullins, James
Swyka, Mildred
Swyka, Nick
Swyka, Pete
Tarabochia, Mary
Tatman, Gary
Terreszcuk, Pete
Thornton, Jane
Titter, Dick
Trush, John
Warwick, Steve
Watson, Mary
Watson, Morrison
Watson, Ralph
Wharton, Charles
Wharton, Clara
Wilcox, Ann
Wilcox, Kenneth
Williams, Frances
Yonko, Mike

Also by Robert Hazel

Books about the Chesapeake and Delaware Canal, featuring historic Chesapeake City, MD

Riding the Ferry and Other Adventures

An Illustrated Collection of Chesapeake City Memories during the Early 1900s.

The Chesapeake and Delaware Canal

An illustrated collection of memories by residents and former residents of Delaware City, Saint Georges, Kirkwood, Summit, and Chesapeake City.

Tales of Uncle Ernest

Chesapeake City, the C&D Canal, and a small farm in the early forties come alive through the eyes of a six-year-old and his dysfunctional uncle.

Times of Uncle Ernest

This is the second of the coming-of-age, Uncle Ernest trilogy. Eavesdrop, as a whimsical character entertains his nephew on lazy afternoons in the forties.

Days of Uncle Ernest

Return to the early forties with a young boy and his story-telling uncle. The setting is a farm near the historic town of Chesapeake City, Maryland. With his bizarre tales, Uncle Ernest entertains an impressionable six-year-old.

Selected Poetry

The Fruitful River in the Eye

Love, humor, and adventure are included in this book of selected poetry.

ROBERT HAZEL
CHESAPEAKE CITY BOOKS
142 N ST AUGUSTINE RD
CHESAPEAKE CITY MD 21915
Email: books4u2@yahoo.com

Made in the USA
Middletown, DE
03 October 2016